ECONOMIC
CHOICES
1987

ECONOMIC CHOICES 1987

Henry J. Aaron
Harvey Galper
Joseph A. Pechman
George L. Perry
Alice M. Rivlin
Charles L. Schultze

THE BROOKINGS INSTITUTION
Washington, D.C.

Foreword

THE HUGE DEFICIT in the federal budget has damaged the ability of U.S. industries to compete in world markets and threatens the long-run health of the economy. In *Economic Choices 1984* a group of Brookings Institution staff members presented a plan to balance the budget by cutting spending and raising taxes. Since then, concern over the deficit has mounted and some progress has been made in reducing it. Nevertheless, the deficit for fiscal 1986 is likely to remain over $200 billion. In desperation, Congress and the president agreed to an extraordinary new procedure for balancing the budget, the Gramm-Rudman-Hollings act.

In this book, six Brookings economists take a new look at the state of the economy, the budget deficit, and the budget process. They present a new plan for reducing the deficit, a plan they believe is preferable to either the proposals made by the Reagan administration or the results of the Gramm-Rudman-Hollings procedures.

Henry J. Aaron, Harvey Galper, Joseph A. Pechman, George L. Perry, and Charles L. Schultze are senior fellows in the Brookings Economic Studies program; Alice M. Rivlin is director of the program. They benefited greatly from frequent consultations with their colleagues at Brookings, especially Alan S. Blinder, Barry P. Bosworth, Ralph C. Bryant, and Robert D. Reischauer. They also received valuable comments from Joseph J. Minarik, John Palmer, Isabel Sawhill, and Charles Stone from the Urban Institute, and from Valerie Amerkhail and Rosemary Marcuss of the Congressional Budget Office.

Research and programming assistance was provided by Charles

R. Byce, Janet L. Chakarian, Charles E. Miles, and John A. Sarich. Secretarial assistance was provided by Ronald J. Bevilac-qua, Dawn R. Emery, Valerie M. Owens, Evelyn M. E. Taylor, Anita Glenn Whitlock, and Kathleen Elliott Yinug. The risk of factual error was minimized by Carolyn A. Rutsch and John A. Sarich. The manuscript was edited by Nancy Davidson, James R. Schneider, and Brenda B. Szittya, and was prepared for typeset-ting by Julie Bailes Legg.

The views expressed are the authors' alone and should not be ascribed to the officers, trustees, or other staff members of the Brookings Institution or to any of those who were consulted or who commented on the manuscript.

BRUCE K. MACLAURY
President

April 1986
Washington, D.C.

Contents

Tables

1

Overview

AFTER four years of frustrating conflict over how to reduce huge federal deficits, in December 1985 Congress passed and the president signed the Balanced Budget and Emergency Deficit Control Act of 1985, better known as the Gramm-Rudman-Hollings act. This peculiar law specifies annual dollar targets that lower the federal deficit to zero by fiscal year 1991. It provides that if Congress and the president fail in any year to agree on a budget whose deficit meets the target, spending will be cut automatically by a formula whose effects, all agree, will damage the effectiveness of both defense and civilian government activities. This state of affairs reflects both the determination of Congress and the president to lower the deficits and their inability to agree how to do it. The law is a budgetary doomsday machine enacted to force the contending parties to come to an agreement in order to avoid the formula cuts that no one wants.

After enactment of the bill, the prospects for lower deficits seemed to brighten. In February the Congressional Budget Office projected annual deficits declining to about $100 billion by fiscal year 1991 without additional spending cuts or tax increases. The estimates contrasted sharply with earlier projections, which showed deficits remaining near $200 billion if policies were not changed. At the same time, interest rates and the value of the dollar were both falling. The press began to report that high deficits were a thing of the past, that they were curing themselves along with the associated symptoms of high interest rates and an overvalued dollar.

This book tries to make sense of these developments. To preview the conclusions briefly, the authors believe that lowering the deficit is still wise policy. Chronic high deficits are damaging to the long-run health of the economy; unless Congress and the president reduce spending or increase taxes or both, deficits will remain high. Moreover, while strict adherence to a specific deficit path is risky, the deficit targets adopted in Gramm-Rudman-Hollings for 1987–89 appear to be both politically attainable and economically sound, given the current state of the economy. The specified downward path of deficits is not likely to be so steep as to precipitate a recession. Indeed, the fall in oil prices and further declines in the value of the dollar and interest rates can be expected to stimulate the economy and offset the restrictive effect of deficit reduction.

There are, however, many ways to reduce the deficit. The formula approach of Gramm-Rudman-Hollings should be avoided. This book explores the implications of three other major budget alternatives: a strategy that would preserve the broad Gramm-Rudman-Hollings priorities but avoid the formula, the administration's proposal, and our own recommended alternative. The last involves smaller spending cuts than the other two and, therefore, requires a tax increase. A tax increase in turn could take different forms, the best of which is an increase in revenue from a reformed income tax.

There is a danger that Congress will be tempted to dally with its doomsday machine by enacting a series of one-shot "gimmicks," such as sales of federal assets or a tax amnesty, that would lower the 1987 deficit enough to avoid triggering automatic cuts. But reliance on such palliatives would leave the underlying deficit and its unwanted economic consequences largely uncorrected. In this book, therefore, we concentrate on measures that would deal with the deficit over the longer run.

Another danger is that Congress and the president will fail to reach agreement on a deficit reduction plan. Such a stalemate could alarm financial markets, send interest rates and the exchange value of the dollar up again, and seriously impair prospects for future growth.

Is the Deficit Disappearing?

In February 1986, the Congressional Budget Office (CBO) issued another in its regular series of reports on what is called the baseline budget, showing estimates of what spending, revenues, and the deficit would be for the next five years if the economy grew at a moderately steady rate and no changes were made in current policy. The report was surprising because it projected baseline deficits declining from $208 billion in fiscal year 1986 to $104 billion in fiscal year 1991, instead of sticking near $200 billion as many observers had expected. At least superficially it looked as though half the battle had been won.

But this conclusion is too optimistic. The fact that the February 1986 baseline deficits were lower than previous estimates reflects a combination of actions already taken and assumptions about the future. First, the significant reductions made by Congress in fiscal year 1986 appropriations, plus the first round of automatic Gramm-Rudman-Hollings cuts that went into effect on March 1, 1986, reduced spending for fiscal year 1986 well below previous expectations. The February CBO baseline assumes that these cuts are not restored. Second, the baseline projections further assume that future defense appropriations grow only enough to compensate for inflation, not at the higher rates assumed in the recent past. Since some of the 1986 cuts will arouse sharp protests, and especially since the president is proposing continued growth in defense outlays after restoration of last year's cuts, it will take strong congressional determination and unity to hold to the CBO baseline. Deficit reduction of the magnitude projected in the baseline will not "just happen."

Why Deficits Should Be Reduced

In fiscal year 1986, federal government spending is likely to be just under $1 trillion, or about 24 percent of the gross national product. The federal government, however, is paying out five dollars for every four it takes in. Federal revenues are about 19 percent of GNP, leaving a deficit of about 5 percent of GNP.

If a deficit of this magnitude were caused by a deep recession, the deficit itself would not be reason for concern. It would serve to cushion the recession and would dwindle as the economy recovered. But the current deficits have persisted in an economy substantially recovered from recession. They are "structural," not temporary, and pose a serious threat to the future growth of the economy.

If an economy is to grow, it must have a high level of investment in plant, equipment, and other forms of capital. To maintain a given level of investment, a nation must either save an equivalent amount from its current income or obtain capital from abroad. National saving is the sum of private and government saving. When the government runs a budget deficit, it "dissaves," and national saving goes down commensurately unless private businesses or individuals increase their saving to make up for the government dissaving. In 1972–81, net national saving in the United States was about 7 percent of gross national product. In 1982–85 it was only about 3 percent. The difference is attributable to the large rise in the budget deficit on top of a slight fall in private saving.

This dearth of national saving has put upward pressure on interest rates and would have cut U.S. investment drastically had it not been for a substantial inflow of capital from abroad. This inflow of foreign funds offers benefits—keeping U.S. interest rates from rising higher, thereby preventing a decline in investment levels—but it also exacts heavy costs. Capital inflow means high foreign demand for dollars and, hence, a high value for the dollar in foreign exchange markets. The expensive dollar, in turn, has impaired the competitiveness of U.S. firms in international markets. Both export industries, including agriculture, and industries competing with imports have found their markets shrinking. The result has been injury to both labor and capital in industries affected by international competition, as well as slower growth of the economy as a whole. If continued over the long run, large budget deficits would either reduce domestic investment or be financed by increasingly uncertain, and potentially reversible, capital inflow from abroad. In either case, living standards of U.S. citizens would fall: a reduced level of domestic investment would retard the growth of the economy, and continued heavy foreign investment would send a larger share of U.S. output abroad in payment of debt service or other returns to foreign investors.

The Road to Gramm-Rudman-Hollings

The structural deficits in the federal budget are the result of actions taken by the president and Congress in 1981, when

Congress enacted the Reagan program of cutting taxes, increasing defense spending, and reducing domestic spending. Domestic spending cuts, however, were not large enough to offset increased defense spending and lower taxes, and most subsequent presidential proposals for additional domestic spending reductions have not been enacted. With the onset of the 1981–82 recession, precipitated by tight money and high interest rates, the actual deficit ballooned still more, and the national debt climbed rapidly. Servicing the larger debt at higher interest rates increased federal interest payments. Even after the economy recovered from the recession, the deficit persisted because federal spending, spurred by increases in defense and interest, was a higher share of GNP than before the recession, and revenues, because of the tax cuts, a lower share.

Although President Reagan won rapid congressional approval of his tax and spending proposals in 1981, the consensus disappeared as the huge deficits emerged. Thereafter, primarily under the leadership of the Senate, the contending parties hammered out painful yearly compromises that halted built-in growth in future deficits but left actual deficits above $200 billion.

The impasse over the budget for fiscal year 1986 dramatized the opposing views. The president's budget proposal, submitted to Congress in February 1985, called for continued defense growth and cuts of over $50 billion in nondefense spending—including wholesale elimination of several programs—aimed at reducing the 1986 deficit to $180 billion. Senate leaders made repeated attempts to work out a compromise plan to reduce the deficit more rapidly by slowing defense growth, broadening domestic cuts to include suspension of social security cost-of-living adjustments, and adding some revenue increases. But in the end they found both the president and the House leadership unwilling to accept such a plan. In late July Congress finally passed a budget resolution that slowed defense growth dramatically and called for smaller domestic cuts than the president had advocated. Congress hoped to reduce the fiscal 1986 deficit to $172 billion but failed to reach agreement on a reconciliation bill implementing many of the domestic spending reductions. That failure, together with unexpectedly slow growth in the economy, crushed all hopes for a fiscal 1986 deficit under $200 billion.

The Gramm-Rudman-Hollings bill passed Congress in the form of an amendment to a bill raising the public debt limit after a protracted struggle over which programs to protect from mandatory cuts. The legislation stipulates that the federal deficit be cut to $172 billion in fiscal year 1986 and $144 billion in 1987, and by $36 billion annually thereafter until it reaches zero in 1991. (For fiscal 1986, the cut was limited by the law to $11.7 billion, even though Congress realized that it was not nearly enough to reach that year's target.) The law instructs the directors of the Office of Management and Budget (OMB) and the Congressional Budget Office to determine, near the beginning of each fiscal year, whether the estimated deficit meets the target. If the deficit exceeds the target by $10 billion, half the excess spending must be cut from the defense budget and the other half from nondefense programs that are not protected. Protected programs include social security and a number of antipoverty programs. Within each category, sufficient reductions must be made in both defense and nondefense spending authority to cut outlays by a uniform percentage. The findings of the OMB and the CBO are transmitted to the comptroller general of the United States, who issues the final report on the cuts required to meet the deficit target. The president is instructed to "sequester" these amounts if an alternative plan has not been worked out with Congress.

Although the legislation had the support of the president and a bipartisan majority in both houses of Congress, the motives and expectations of the actors in this ongoing legislative drama differ widely. The president hopes to force Congress to accept his proposals to eliminate a number of nondefense programs and reduce outlays in others while continuing the defense buildup. Many members of Congress, including ranking Republicans, have already given notice that they will not support many of the nondefense outlay cuts sought by the president and will seek major cuts in his proposed defense outlays. Many lawmakers believe that the president must ultimately accept a tax increase in order to preserve his defense policy.

On February 7, 1986, a panel of three judges from the U.S. District Court for the District of Columbia ruled that because the Gramm-Rudman-Hollings bill grants executive powers to the comptroller general, who is an officer removable by Congress, it violates the principle of separation of powers in the U.S. Constitution. The ruling has been appealed to the Supreme Court. In anticipation of just such a ruling, the bill provides a fallback procedure under which the mandatory cuts would be implemented if the House and Senate passed a joint resolution approving the mandatory cuts, but the resolution must be signed by the president. Regardless of how the Supreme Court rules on procedure, both the president and Congress are under pressure to meet the deficit targets of the legislation.

Will Rapid Deficit Reduction Cause Recession?

The case for reducing the deficits is powerful, and the new budget law symbolizes the determination of Congress and the president to reduce them. It would, of course, be foolish to cut the deficit so rapidly that the economy plunges into recession, but several sources of economic strength make 1986 a good year to start deficit reduction. The stimulating effects of low interest rates and further declines in the value of the dollar are likely to offset the restrictive effects of following the targeted deficit reductions in the period 1987–89.

After slowing in 1985 and early 1986, growth in the economy seems likely to pick up later in 1986. Partly in response to the prospect of declining deficits, interest rates have come down and stock market prices have climbed rapidly in recent months. Lower interest rates and reduced costs of raising equity capital should stimulate both the housing market and investment. The substantial drop in the exchange value of the dollar from its peak in the first quarter of 1985 should stimulate net exports and increase output and employment in U.S. industries that compete in world markets. The rising cost of imports will add somewhat to inflation in the United States, but another favorable development—the rapid slide in oil prices—will have the opposite effect. Oil prices have fallen precipitously from their 1985 level of $27 a barrel. Even if they stabilize around $20 a barrel instead of a possible $10 to $15 a barrel, consumer prices will be reduced about 1 percent, real incomes will be up, and consumer demand strengthened. On the negative side, investment in the oil industry will be cut sharply, and the risk of defaults on loans to oil-exporting countries and to the domestic oil industry will grow. On balance, however, lower oil prices enhance the chances that the economy will grow strongly enough in 1986 to absorb deficit reduction without slowing.

Estimating the effect of reaching the deficit targets in 1987–89, of course, involves considerably more uncertainty. Reducing the structural deficit by 2.6 percent of GNP from 1986 through 1989, which is what the new budget law requires, would clearly have a major restrictive effect on the economy if not offset by some other stimulus. The most likely source of offsetting stimulus is a reduction in the current account deficit. Whether this stimulus is sufficiently large depends in turn on how much further the value of the dollar falls and how fast the economies of U.S. trading partners grow.

U.S. monetary authorities can be expected to try to keep the U.S. economy growing at about 3.5 percent a year as the budget deficit comes down. On the assumptions that the dollar falls 15 percent a year (from its level in January 1986) through 1988 and that foreign economies also grow at 3.5 percent a year, the U.S. current account deficit can be expected to shrink steadily, perhaps disappearing entirely by 1990. Under these conditions—which seem quite possible—the improved competitiveness of U.S. industry should stimulate the economy enough to offset the restrictive effect of budget deficit reduction. Slower growth abroad or smaller declines in the dollar would provide less offsetting stimulus. Much depends, therefore, on the willingness of foreign governments to expand their own economies and, especially, not to impede further readjustment of the dollar. If the dollar were to stay at its early 1986 levels, stimulus from net exports would be much smaller, even with strong growth abroad.

Should the Budget Be Balanced in 1991?

If the economy continues to grow steadily and the deficit targets are achieved, the federal deficit will be $72 billion, or 1.3 percent of GNP, in 1989. Is that good enough, or should it be reduced to zero as Gramm-Rudman-Hollings prescribes? It is too soon to tell.

Reducing the deficit to zero would increase national saving to about 8.5 percent of GNP if private saving did not change. Would sufficient investment opportunities be available to absorb that much saving? The answer again dramatizes the importance of the future behavior of the dollar and the current account balance. If the dollar falls sufficiently, the current account deficit will disappear and the United States can resume its historical role of modest net investor in the rest of the world. Sufficient investment opportunities would then probably be available to absorb the savings. The situation would be similar to many other high-employment years in the past. If net capital inflow continued at recent rates while the deficit went to zero, however, the United States would be overwhelmed with savings—its own and other nations'—for which domestic investment opportunities are unlikely to exist. In this case, balancing the budget would cause a weak economy.

Avoiding Doomsday

The first practical consequence of Gramm-Rudman-Hollings was the sequestration of $11.7 billion in fiscal 1986 spending that took effect on March 1, 1986. Since the amount was relatively small and the fiscal year was nearly half over, Congress decided to let the automatic sequestration process take effect rather than try to reach agreement on alternative cuts. After exempt and specially treated programs were set aside, reducing outlays by $11.7 billion turned out to require cutting appropriations for defense by 4.9 percent and unprotected domestic programs by 4.3 percent. The difficulties of reducing ongoing programs by even such small percentages in midyear gave government agencies reason to hope that sequestration would not be repeated.

Indeed, almost everyone agrees that reaching the deficit targets by applying the sequestration formula in future years would introduce major distortions and inefficiencies into government activities. If, for example, the targets were reached by applying the sequestration formula to the CBO baseline projection for 1987–89, real defense spending would have to be $18 billion lower in 1989 than in 1986. Moreover, each line item would have to be cut by the same percentage, leaving no room for military judgment about whether certain items were more vital than others. Similarly, on the civilian side the automatic formula would be applied equally, and indiscriminately, to air traffic controllers, IRS auditors, and the national zoo. The sequestration results applied to 1987 and beyond clearly constitute, as intended, an alternative to be avoided. There must be a better way to reduce the deficits.

Three Alternative Budget Strategies

Reducing the budget deficit to meet the Gramm-Rudman-Hollings targets will require critical decisions about broad national priorities.

—How much of the deficit reduction should be realized through spending cuts and how much through tax increases?

—Of the spending cuts, how much should be in defense and how much in civilian programs?

—Should social security and related entitlement programs share in the cuts?

—In other programs, should the cuts be evenly distributed, or should they be highly selective?

This book examines the implications of three budget reduction "packages," each of which answers these questions in a different way. The first is the one broadly suggested by the Gramm-Rudman-Hollings law; the second is the president's. We propose a third.

Gramm-Rudman-Hollings Priorities

While everyone agrees that application of the sequestration formula in the new budget law would be devastating, the broad outlines of Gramm-Rudman-Hollings reflect the realities of the political environment in which it was shaped and therefore represent a feasible budget strategy. Such a strategy would avoid a tax increase, which many in Congress are certainly reluctant to support, especially over presidential opposition. It would also exempt social security and certain programs for the poor from mandatory cuts and give special treatment to other health and retirement programs. And it would divide the remaining cuts between defense and the unprotected domestic programs, a kind of rough justice reflecting a political compromise between those who give highest priority to national security and those who believe the defense buildup has gone far enough.

The Administration's Proposal

The budget proposal presented by the president in February 1986 reflects quite a different approach. The president would achieve some of the reduction in the deficit through the sale of public assets and several small tax increases. He would leave social security benefits untouched, but make substantial reductions in other programs that would be wholly or partially protected under Gramm-Rudman-Hollings, especially medicare, medicaid, and student aid. He requests restoration of most of the $14 billion cut from defense budget authority in 1986 and proposes increases of 3 percent a year over inflation in subsequent years. The bulk of deficit reduction is accomplished by deep but highly selective cuts in the unprotected civilian programs, including outright abolition of a number of programs.

The Recommended Alternative

Reaching the 1989 Gramm-Rudman-Hollings deficit target solely by cutting spending poses unnecessarily grim choices. Slashing defense spending as much as would be required under the package that preserves Gramm-Rudman-Hollings priorities would be risky to national security. After the recent rapid modernization of military equipment, reducing defense budgets substantially below current levels would lead to unbalanced forces with sophisticated equipment and insufficient funds to operate and maintain it effectively. Deep cuts in civilian programs would curtail important government services. Programs that hardly anyone regards as wasteful—scientific research, medical care for low-income people, job training, and maintenance of the nation's highways and bridges—would be cut. It would be preferable to raise taxes by about $50 billion, or about 1 percent of GNP, in 1989. We propose, therefore, an alternative budget that would hold the defense budget at fiscal year 1986 levels with allowance for inflation, accept some of the cuts proposed by the president, spread the burden of deficit reduction more broadly (to include, for example, social security beneficiaries), and restore some funds in programs cut too deeply already.

Table 1-1. *Comparison of Alternative Strategies for Deficit Reduction, Fiscal Year 1989*
Billions of dollars

Item	GRH	Adminis-tration[a]	Recom-mended
Baseline deficit (before GRH 1986 cuts;			
3 percent defense growth)	187	187	187
Spending changes	−115	−105	−65
Defense	−56	−4	−29
Civilian	−44	−77	−21
Cuts	−44	−79	−30
Selected increases	0	2	9
Interest	−15	−15	−15
Asset sales	0	−9	0
Revenue changes	0	−9	−50
New deficit	72	72	72

Sources: Congressional Budget Office; and authors' estimates. Numbers are rounded.
a. Includes additional cuts needed to offset administration underestimates of expenditures (see chap. 3).

The changes in taxes and spending under each of the three alternatives in fiscal year 1989 are compared in table 1-1. The table shows changes from the baseline deficit for 1989 calculated before the enactment of Gramm-Rudman-Hollings in the fall of 1985. At that time, using current CBO economic assumptions but projecting a 3 percent real growth in defense, one would have estimated a 1989 deficit of about $187 billion. Each alternative would reduce the deficit to about $72 billion in 1989 but do it in a very different way. Table 1-2 compares major types of revenue and spending under the three alternatives as a percentage of GNP in 1989 and in earlier years.

The president proposes to continue to increase defense spending rapidly during the next five years, and would meet the Gramm-Rudman-Hollings targets by cutting nondefense spending sharply. Real defense outlays in 1989 would be 8 percent higher than in 1986 and 51 percent higher than in 1981. Since the president opposes tax increases, all the deficit reductions except the extension of the cigarette tax and increases in user charges come from cuts in nondefense programs, and these would be substantial.

Table 1-2. *Trends in Selected Components of Federal Revenues and Outlays, Fiscal Years 1960–69 and 1981, and under Three Alternative Budget Programs, Fiscal Year 1989*
Percent of GNP

			1989		
Component	1960–69	1981	GRH[a]	Adminis-tration[b]	Recom-mended
Revenues	18.2	20.1	19.0	19.2	20.0
General	15.5	14.6	12.7	12.9	13.7
Social security[c]	2.7	5.5	6.3	6.3	6.3
Outlays	19.0	22.7	20.4	20.6	21.3
Defense	8.9	5.3	5.4	6.4	6.0
Net interest	1.3	2.3	2.9	2.9	2.9
Social security[d]	2.8	6.1	6.6	6.4	6.4
Other	6.0	9.0	5.6	4.9	6.0

Sources: *Historical Tables, Budget of the United States Government, Fiscal Year 1987;* CBO, *The Economic and Budget Outlook: Fiscal Years 1987–1991* (CBO, 1986); and authors' estimates.

a. Assumes cuts are made from a baseline that incorporates zero real growth in defense budget authority.

b. Assumes additional civilian spending cuts sufficient to substitute for asset sales and to offset spending underestimates.

c. Includes hospital insurance tax.

d. Includes medicare outlays.

Social security benefits would remain untouched, but other programs that are partially or wholly protected under Gramm-Rudman-Hollings, as well as the unprotected programs, would feel the effects of the cuts. Outlays of all protected programs, including social security, would remain the same in real terms between 1986 and 1989, while those of unprotected programs would be 27 percent lower in 1989 than in 1986 and 33 percent lower than in 1981. Although the president has proposed some sensible cuts and reforms in various programs, his continued commitment to defense growth and opposition to a tax increase force him to subject social programs to cuts that are both excessive and politically unacceptable. As a share of GNP, spending for domestic programs other than social security would fall well below the levels of the 1960s.

The Gramm-Rudman-Hollings package is equally untenable,

but for different reasons. Under this option, 29 percent of the defense buildup from 1981 to 1986 would be reversed by 1989. Real defense spending would be 8 percent lower in 1989 than in 1986. Such cuts would introduce major distortions into the nation's military operations and weaken the readiness of the armed forces.

The cuts in the nondefense programs under this package would also introduce major distortions and inequities. Since much of the civilian budget is spared from the full force of the cuts under Gramm-Rudman-Hollings, the remaining cuts, concentrated in a small segment of the budget, have to be deep indeed. By 1989, total outlays of the unprotected civilian programs would be cut 28 percent below the 1981 levels in real terms. But Congress would not tolerate cuts of this magnitude in essential federal programs such as tax collection and enforcement by the Internal Revenue Service, aviation traffic control and safety by the Federal Aviation Administration, and the safety program of the Nuclear Regulatory Commission. Hence, the necessary cuts in the remaining civilian activities of the federal government would be even more drastic.

Our recommended alternative requires a tax increase of $50 billion in 1989 to help alleviate the unacceptable consequences of the other two options. Such a tax increase would keep the GNP share of general revenue—that is, revenue other than payroll taxes for social security and medicare—below the level in 1981. Yet it would be sufficient to avoid cuts that would weaken the nation's defense and undermine the ability of the federal government to perform essential public services and to provide support for the poor and disadvantaged. Real defense spending would be the same in fiscal 1989 as in 1986 and would support a strong defense posture. Real outlays of unprotected nondefense programs would decline 10 percent between 1986 and 1989, but the cuts would be concentrated in low-priority programs.

It should be emphasized that the outlay estimates under all three options assume that budget decisions for fiscal 1987 and beyond will begin with the spending levels mandated under the Gramm-Rudman-Hollings sequestration procedures that went into effect on March 1, 1986. These cuts reduced budget outlays by $18 billion in fiscal 1987, $21 billion in 1988, and $23 billion in 1989. Any spending above these levels would require equal

Table 1-3. *Alternative Revenue Sources, Fiscal Years 1987–91*
Billions of dollars

	Income tax[a]		Excise tax[b]			
Year	Rate increase (2 percentage points)	Surtax (9 percent)	Oil[c]	Gasoline[d]	Alcohol and tobacco[e]	Value-added tax (4 percent)[f]
1987	33.2	32.4	20.4	25.6	6.8	...
1988	47.7	46.3	21.8	25.6	9.5	33.9
1989	52.4	50.9	22.1	25.6	9.6	51.3
1990	57.0	55.6	22.5	25.2	9.6	55.2
1991	62.1	60.8	22.9	24.9	9.6	59.4

Sources: Congressional Budget Office; and authors' estimates.
a. Includes individual and corporation income taxes. Based on H.R. 3838 as enacted by the House of Representatives.
b. Assumes increases would be effective October 1, 1986.
c. Tax of $5 a barrel on domestic and imported oil.
d. Tax increase of 30 cents a gallon.
e. Increase cigarette tax to 32 cents a pack and double tax on alcohol. Assumes scheduled reduction of cigarette tax from 16 cents to 8 cents a pack on March 15, 1986.
f. Includes exemptions for food, housing, and medical care. Assumes effective date of January 1, 1988.

offsetting cuts in other programs or a larger tax increase than the $50 billion provided in our preferred option.

Tax Options

The question of which taxes to raise to help meet the Gramm-Rudman-Hollings deficit targets, and by how much, is complicated by still another policy debate—tax reform. With the strong support of the president, Congress is now considering an overhaul of the personal and corporation income taxes. The goal is to broaden the bases of these income taxes by eliminating tax preferences and to apply the extra revenue to reduction of marginal tax rates. The question is how the objective of tax reform—a fairer tax system—can be wedded to the goal of reducing the deficit.

Congress can address this issue in one of three ways, as shown in table 1-3. First, the tax reform bill already passed by the House of Representatives (H.R. 3838) could be modified to raise more income tax revenues than are produced under present law. Congressional leaders must decide whether to raise those revenues in the reform bill or in separate legislation. Second, selective excise taxes on consumer goods could be increased. Higher taxes on petroleum products, alcoholic beverages, and tobacco products, which enjoy lower tax rates in the United States than they do in most other countries, would not only raise revenues but advance other objectives as well. For example, increased taxes on oil or gasoline would encourage energy conservation, and higher taxes on distilled spirits, wine, beer, and cigarettes could reduce consumption of products that are injurious to health. Third, Congress could enact a new broad-based consumption tax. The two leading alternatives are a federal retail sales tax or a value-added tax. The major difference is administrative; the sales tax is collected only at the retail stage, while the value-added tax is collected at all stages of production. Such taxes are potentially large revenue producers and could be used to finance some of the rate reductions in the tax reform bill as well as to increase federal revenues.

We believe that the best instruments for raising the revenues necessary to reach the Gramm-Rudman-Hollings targets are the individual and corporation income taxes. These taxes are imposed at rates that reflect social judgments about ability to pay and are designed to take into account the economic circumstances of taxpaying units. Consumption taxes, whether levied on selected commodities or on a broad base, would impose heavier burdens on poor and low-income families than on those higher up in the income scale.

Income tax revenues can be raised by broadening the tax base further or by making smaller rate cuts than are now contemplated in the House bill. Additional potential base-broadening measures include limitations on the amount or types of employee fringe benefits that are excluded from tax, an increase in the proportion of social security benefits that is taxed, or limitation of the deductibility of state and local taxes on individual federal income tax returns.

Political opposition to these changes may mean that additional revenues will have to come mainly from rate increases. Income tax rates can be increased in two simple ways. All tax rates can be increased by the same number of percentage points, or all tax payments can be increased by the same percentage. A 2 percentage point increase in the individual and corporation tax rates or a 9 percent surtax would raise somewhat more than the $50 billion revenue increase proposed by our recommended alternative to reach the deficit target for 1989. If H.R. 3838 survives in anything like its present form, such rate increases should be more acceptable than they would have been without tax reform.

Among the excise taxes, the largest potential revenue producers are those on oil and gasoline. A tax of $5 a gallon on imported oil would raise about $7.5 billion in fiscal 1989; the same tax on domestic as well as imported oil would generate $22 billion. Both taxes would boost prices, but the entire price increase would go into the federal Treasury under the general oil tax, while the import tax would siphon off most of it to domestic producers. A gasoline tax of 30 cents a gallon would raise about $26 billion in 1989 and would prevent declines in gasoline prices that might undermine consumers' incentives for owning fuel-efficient cars.

Excise taxes on tobacco products and alcoholic beverages have declined in real terms in the last three decades because they have not kept up with inflation. Doubling liquor taxes by 1989 would restore these taxes to their real levels in 1973; increasing cigarette taxes to 32¢ a pack would restore them to their real levels in 1958. Together, these increases would boost revenues by almost $10 billion in 1989. The additional taxes would require heavy consumers of such products to pay an extra share of the costs they impose on society for health care. Reasonable increases in excise taxes could add from $15 billion to $30 billion to federal revenues in 1989.

Broad-based consumption taxes are capable of producing a great deal of revenue at low rates. A retail sales tax or value-added tax that exempts food, housing, and medical care would raise about $12.5 billion for each percentage point of tax in 1989. Thus a tax rate of 4 percent would meet the revenue target of $50 billion for that year. But because of the delays of introducing a new tax, it would be necessary to resort to other revenue increases to meet the 1987 and 1988 targets. In our view, Congress should turn to such a tax only if it becomes clear that the needed revenues cannot be raised from the income and excise taxes.

Improving the Budget Process

The impasse over the deficit has put great strains on the process by which the U.S. government makes budget decisions. Budget making is always difficult, particularly when power is divided, as it is under the Constitution, between the president and Congress. For the last several years the president and Congress have held divergent views about how to reduce the deficits and have displayed only limited willingness to compromise. Progress toward lower deficits has been slow and painful.

It seems unlikely that any changes in budget-making procedures could have ameliorated this political conflict. Unless the United States is willing to give up the constitutional separation of powers and move toward a parliamentary system—a move for which the authors have little enthusiasm—there will occasionally be times when Congress and the president disagree.

The enactment of Gramm-Rudman-Hollings reflected the mutual frustration of Congress and the president over their inability to agree on a plan to reduce deficits. They hoped that by agreeing in advance to cut spending in ways no one regarded as desirable, they would force themselves to compromise on a more sensible way to reduce the deficit.

While the new budget law may have the intended effect of forcing an agreement, it is still a bad way to make a budget and should be repealed. Aiming for any fixed dollar target for the deficit—such as zero in fiscal year 1991—without regard for the state of the economy could force the government to adopt fiscal policy that would undermine the economy's health. Moreover, cutting deficits by formula rather than by deliberate consideration of relative priorities is an abdication of responsible decision-making.

The stress of the deficit problem has also exacerbated a long-standing problem of the budget process: its unnecessary complexity. The U.S. government makes budget decisions too often, in too many stages, and in too great detail.

The budget process should be greatly simplified. Most spending decisions should be made for more than a year at a time; indeed, the whole budget should be shifted to a biennial basis. The authorization and appropriation functions, which are now exercised by separate committees in both the House and the Senate, should be combined. The number of line items in the budget should be greatly reduced, and Congress should pay less attention to minor details of the budget and more attention to major policy issues.

Procedural reforms can make budgeting more comprehensible and the process less time consuming, but they cannot make the decisions easier. Budget decisions, especially the painful ones that are required to close a deficit, will always involve hard economic and political choices. Resolving them requires patience, a willingness to compromise, leadership, and political will.

2

Economic Policy

IN ADDRESSING the issues raised by the Gramm-Rudman-Hollings law, it is important to consider four related questions: What effect does a large federal budget deficit have on the economy? Is legislating a predetermined path for deficit reduction a safe way to set budget policy? Even as a tentative goal, is the path mandated by Gramm-Rudman-Hollings so steep that it will throw the economy into recession? And should this deficit reduction path be followed all the way to a balanced budget in 1991?

We conclude that while a federal deficit is often appropriate, the recent and current large federal deficits and the high real interest rates associated with them have been harmful to the economy. If a political stalemate were to prevent major deficit reductions from being implemented, serious damage to the economy could result. However, important as deficit reduction is, it is wrong to enforce a path of deficit reduction for the future without regard for the underlying strength of the economy. In an uncertain world, a fixed deficit path is inherently destabilizing and could cause or deepen a recession or retard a recovery.

Although it is important to maintain flexibility in setting future budgets, we believe that the economy is now robust enough to absorb substantial deficit reductions. Taken as a tentative goal, the Gramm-Rudman-Hollings target deficits for 1987–89 are unlikely to affect the economy adversely if, as seems probable, the exchange value of the dollar declines further and if, as will be necessary, the Federal Reserve follows an appropriately flexible monetary policy. As for the years beyond 1989, it is too soon to say whether attaining a balanced budget by 1991 would be overly restrictive.

Deficits, Domestic Saving, and Foreign Investment

A deficit in the federal budget is not always harmful to the economy. Indeed, it may help cushion a recession and stimulate economic growth. When the economy slides into recession, tax revenues fall off and some unemployment-related spending rises. Thus a recession automatically causes or increases a deficit in the federal budget. As the economy returns to high employment, a recession-related deficit will disappear. Attempts to reduce a recession-induced deficit by raising taxes or cutting spending will reduce income and make the recession deeper.

A deficit that would remain even if the economy were growing along a high-employment path is called a structural or high-employment deficit. About two-thirds of the current federal budget deficit of over $200 billion or nearly 5 percent of GNP is structural, because it persists even after the economy has recovered substantially from the deep recession of 1981–82. A structural deficit of this size is both costly and risky for the U.S. economy.

Large continuing deficits in times of prosperity are costly because they reduce national saving and the future returns to that saving. The reduction in saving either forces a reduction in investment in the United States or finances that investment with funds from abroad. Either effect reduces the growth of income for residents of the United States. If investment in the United States remains strong because foreigners invest here or because U.S. firms borrow abroad, the United States must import more than it exports. Markets achieve that result by increasing the value of the dollar relative to foreign currencies. The result is reduced competitiveness of U.S. goods that trade on world markets. Thus whether U.S. investment falls or is maintained by financing from abroad, the result is unexpected losses of jobs and profits in sectors that produce tradable goods or investment goods or both.

Long-run growth depends on the accumulation of capital, which in turn depends on the rate of national saving. As table 2-1 shows, historical variations in U.S. net national saving have been closely linked to the federal government's surplus or deficit. Major tax cuts and a large defense buildup boosted the federal deficit to an

Table 2-1. *Saving and Investment Flows, 1954–85* [a]
Percent of GNP

Period or year	Federal surplus	+	Net private saving	+	State and local surplus	=	Net national saving	=	Net domestic investment	+	Net foreign investment
1954–61	−0.2		7.1		−0.2		6.7		6.2		0.5
1962–71	−0.6		8.0		0.1		7.5		7.1		0.4
1972–81	−1.9		7.8		1.0		6.9		6.6		0.3
1982–85	−4.9		6.3		1.4		2.8		4.4		−1.6
1982	−4.6		5.5		1.1		2.0		2.0		0.0
1983	−5.3		5.9		1.4		2.1		3.0		−0.9
1984	−4.6		7.3		1.7		4.4		6.8		−2.4
1985	−5.0		6.4		1.5		2.9		5.8		−2.9

Sources: U.S. Department of Commerce, Bureau of Economic Analysis, *The National Income and Product Accounts of the United States, 1929–1982 Statistical Tables* (Government Printing Office, forthcoming), and *Survey of Current Business*, vol. 66 (March 1986). Figures are rounded.
a. The statistical discrepancy in the national income accounts is assumed to be zero.

average of 4.9 percent of GNP in 1982–85. At the same time, net national saving declined by more than half its 1972–81 level to an average of 2.8 percent of GNP. In 1982–83 national saving was depressed in part because a slack economy enlarged federal deficits and reduced business saving. But even in 1984 and 1985, when the economy was near its average utilization rate, net national saving remained well below the rates experienced from 1954 to 1981. This low rate of saving, in turn, was accompanied by very high real rates of interest. During 1982–85 the real interest rate on three-month Treasury bills (nominal rates less the annual rate of inflation in the GNP deflator) averaged 4.5 percent, 3 percentage points above the rates in 1960–79. Real interest rates on long-term government bonds averaged 4.5 percentage points more than in 1960–79.

National saving equals the sum of domestic and foreign investment. If national saving falls, investment at home or abroad must also fall. Because the exchange value of the dollar rose between 1980 and 1985 and because very generous tax incentives for domestic investment were enacted in 1981, most of the decrease in the national saving rate has come through a decline in the net foreign investment rate. In 1985 the flow of foreign investments to the United States exceeded the flow of U.S. investments abroad by $115 billion, or 2.9 percent of GNP. The net inflow of foreign funds kept U.S. interest rates from being even higher than they were and permitted domestic investment as a share of GNP to remain near the historical level. However, in light of the tax incentives that were provided, this level of domestic investment was disappointing.

Although domestic investment has been sustained by the inflow of foreign funds, the damage to future income growth from depressed national saving is much the same as it would have been if budget deficits had crowded out domestic investment. If there had been no investment, there would be no returns to distribute. With investments owned by foreigners or financed by foreign capital, production inside the United States increases, but most of the returns flow abroad to the foreign investors. In neither case can future U.S. consumption grow at the higher rate that would be possible with higher U.S. national saving.

Negative net foreign investment corresponds to a deficit in U.S. current account transactions with foreigners. The United States imports more goods and services than it exports by borrowing the difference from foreigners. Last year's $115 billion current account deficit arose largely because the value of the dollar rose sharply between 1980 and 1985, reducing the competitiveness of U.S. goods on world markets.

This decline in international competitiveness has hurt many U.S. industries, but it has also produced some temporary benefits. The strong dollar has reduced inflation, both by reducing U.S. prices of imported goods and by depressing wages and prices in U.S. industries that compete with foreign goods either in this country or abroad. By making foreign goods cheaper to buy, the strong dollar has also enhanced U.S. real incomes.

Those gains will be lost, however, as the dollar depreciates. Moreover, although lower prices from a strong dollar have helped consumers in the short run, they have also depressed profits and employment in sectors of the economy most susceptible to foreign competition, thereby reducing the value of capital investment there, including the value of agricultural land. The markets that have been lost because the dollar has been so strong will not be easily regained even when the dollar returns to a lower level sustainable over the longer run, because foreigners have invested heavily in competing industries abroad.

The current reliance on funds borrowed from foreigners raises risks of instability in the future, especially if U.S. budget deficits are not reduced. Current trade deficits are not sustainable. In 1985 the United States became a net debtor nation. The size of the net external debt will grow by roughly the amount of each year's current account deficit, projected to rise to about $130 billion in 1986. At this rate, U.S. net external debt would reach over $400 billion by the time President Reagan leaves office. But foreigners may be unwilling to lend the United States that much. If their desire to accumulate dollar assets lessens, the dollar would have to depreciate to a level consistent with a smaller deficit or a surplus in the current account. And if U.S. budget deficits are still large at that time, interest rates in the United States would have to rise in order to squeeze out domestic investment.

In this last event, the Federal Reserve would face the delicate task of permitting just enough tightening in financial markets to slow investment without simultaneously causing recession. The risk of error—and of recession—would be acute. Thus inaction on the budget deficit, which requires a continued massive inflow of foreign funds to sustain investment, poses serious risks to economic stability. If U.S. budget deficits are reduced now, the inevitable adjustment of the exchange rate and current account can ease the economic transition to lower deficits rather than cause problems. The dollar began to decline after March 1985, in part because investors came to expect that U.S. budget deficits would be reduced and U.S. interest rates would decline. That combination of events maximizes the chances of a smooth transition, as we show below.

Deficit Reduction and the Economy

The case for reducing the deficit is powerful. But excessively rapid cuts could reduce demand faster than could be offset by the beneficial effects of lower deficits on interest and exchange rates. Is the pace of deficit cuts required by Gramm-Rudman-Hollings achievable without threatening economic slowdown? The answer to that question is a cautious "yes"—at least through 1989.

The Near-Term Outlook

If budget deficits are going to be cut, the right time is when other developments can be expected to add strength to the expansion, offsetting the decline in fiscal stimulus. The budget will become more restrictive during 1986. The sequestration of funds that began in spring 1986 has already started to reduce fiscal stimulus to the economy by about $20 billion at an annual rate. And larger cuts will come in the fall if the Gramm-Rudman-Hollings targets are met.

But credit markets have responded to the promise of fiscal restraint. The budget debate of 1985 caused financial analysts to lower their estimates of the size of future deficits. As a result, long-term interest rates fell nearly 2.5 percentage points between June 1985 and mid-March 1986. The average price of equities rose 28 percent over this period.

Lower interest rates and higher stock market prices will encourage housing construction and other forms of investment. In addition, both the anticipation of reduced deficits and the associated decline in interest rates have helped reduce the exchange value of the dollar, which will help to increase exports and reduce imports. The sharp reduction in world oil prices may cut into the expansion early in the year, but should add to growth as the year goes on.

Thus after a slow start, it seems likely that real GNP will grow at a satisfactory rate in 1986, with help from an easing monetary policy. Unemployment is projected to decline, and consumer prices are likely to continue to rise at a moderate rate.

The Impact of Oil Prices

Oil prices fell sharply in early 1986 because production exceeded world demand by 2 million to 3 million barrels a day. The course of oil prices depends crucially on whether OPEC and other producers successfully collude to restrain production. If they fail, effective transaction prices could fall to the recent low levels of auction prices and remain low, perhaps as little as $10 to $15 a barrel. If collusion should succeed, prices could exceed $20 a barrel.

Because the two major increases in oil prices in 1973–74 and 1979–80 were associated with massive worldwide recessions, it may be tempting to infer that the present break in oil prices will generate a worldwide boom. But the symmetry is far from perfect.

The recessions that followed increases in oil prices were caused by the reactions of monetary authorities as well as by the direct effects of higher oil prices themselves. Governments in most industrial nations were already acutely concerned about inflation even before oil prices rose. Accommodating the oil price increases so as to maintain real output growth threatened to create a big jump in inflation. Authorities in various countries chose to maintain restrictive monetary policies, thereby contributing to the deep and long-lived recessions.

The 1986 fall in oil prices will permit decisionmakers to expand demand with less concern that expansionary actions will trigger inflation, but it will not force them to do so. It is most likely to encourage more expansionary policies outside the United States, especially in Europe, where recovery from the deep recessions brought on by the 1979–80 oil shocks has been inadequate. Unemployment remains at 10 percent or more in several countries. In addition, rising currency values in some of these countries will help hold down inflation during expansion.

In the United States, the situation is somewhat different. The favorable effects of falling oil prices on U.S. inflation will offset the unfavorable price effects of dollar depreciation. Unemployment in 1986 may approach levels that the Federal Reserve regards as a trip wire for wage inflation; and the economy was already expanding adequately before the oil price break. In this situation the Federal Reserve is unlikely to adopt a much more expansionary monetary policy unless economic activity slackens.

A decline in oil prices from $27 a barrel in 1985 will affect many aspects of economic performance. Even a drop to $20 will directly reduce the nation's oil import bill by about $10 billion and will cut about 1 percentage point from the year's increase in the consumer price index. Wage growth will slow down by only a small fraction of this cut in consumer prices. So the 1 percent cut in the CPI will translate into an almost corresponding increase in real personal income and will contribute to strength in real consumer demand. A greater decline in oil prices will magnify these favorable effects correspondingly.

The same oil price drop that helps consumers, however, hurts producers and creates problems for their creditors. Investment in development and exploration of oil fields will be cut sharply, especially with oil prices near their levels of early 1986. This will reduce GNP growth in the early part of the year. Exports to oil-producing nations will decline as their oil revenues fall and they curtail imports from the United States and other countries; this unfavorable effect will partially offset the favorable consequences of lower oil prices for the U.S. trade balance.

Banks with loans to Mexico, Venezuela, and other nations heavily dependent on oil exports for foreign exchange will confront an increasing prospect of losses on those loans. So will financial institutions with loans tied to domestic drilling and exploration and to related real estate. The severity of these financial problems will grow disproportionately with the size of the oil price decline.

On balance, in the United States lower oil prices will help offset the effects of a weakening dollar on price levels and, later in 1986, will help offset the restrictive effects of a tightening budget on output. But they do not promise an economic boom and they do raise the likelihood of financial problems.

The Exchange Value of the Dollar

The transition from a rising to a falling exchange value of the dollar began in 1985. The rate of decline of the dollar has been spectacular, measured either from September 1985, when the Group of Five finance ministers announced their joint view that the dollar ought to depreciate, or from the dollar's peak in the first quarter of 1985 (see table 2-2). However, the dollar's recent value against an average of all major foreign currencies was still sub-stantially above the levels prevailing in 1979–80.[1] These exchange rate developments have two implications for the economy in the near term.

First, the dollar's depreciation does not yet have significant consequences for the domestic price level. The dollar's peak in the first quarter of 1985 was brief, and most import prices never reflected it. Furthermore, foreign profit margins had widened in response to the dollar's appreciation and have since absorbed part of the subsequent depreciation. Despite the dollar's fall, therefore,

---

1. Table 2-2 reports changes in nominal exchange rates. Real (inflation-adjusted) exchange rates have moved similarly, rising dramatically from 1980 to the first quarter of 1985 and falling sharply since then.

Table 2-2. *Changes in Exchange Value of the Dollar between February 28, 1986, and Selected Earlier Dates, 1979–85*
Percent

	Change to February 28						
Currency measure	1979–80 average	1981	1982	1983	1984	1985:1	September 20, 1985[a]
Yen	− 19	− 18	− 28	− 24	− 24	− 30	− 25
Deutsche mark	22	− 1	− 8	− 13	− 22	− 32	− 22
Multilateral average[b]	31	12	− 1	− 8	− 17	− 26	− 18
Bilateral average[c]	20	10	− 1	− 4	− 11	− 19	− 13

Sources: Board of Governors of the Federal Reserve System, *Federal Reserve Bulletin*, various issues; and Morgan Guaranty Trust, *World Financial Markets*, various issues.

a. The Friday before the September 22, 1985, meeting in New York of the finance ministers and central bank governors of the Group of Five countries.

b. Federal Reserve series for the weighted-average nominal exchange value of the U.S. dollar against the currencies of the Group of Ten industrial countries. Individual exchange rates are weighted by the shares of countries in the total (global) trade of all countries in the group.

c. Morgan Guaranty series for the weighted-average nominal exchange value of the U.S. dollar against the currencies of fifteen major industrial countries. Individual exchange rates are weighted by the shares of countries in U.S. trade with the group of countries.

import prices did not change between the beginning and end of 1985. By later this year, however, the lower dollar will start adding modestly to the U.S. price level, perhaps offsetting the effect of lower oil prices for the year as a whole.

Second, since competitiveness depends on relative prices, the dollar's movement has had little effect on the U.S. trade balance as of early 1986. But as the year progresses, the effects of the lower dollar, together with quickening expansions abroad, should start improving the trade balance, providing a boost to the economic expansion. With further declines in the dollar, this improvement will continue in 1987 and beyond.

Deficit Reduction in 1987–89

The major stabilization question surrounding the budget is whether meeting the Gramm-Rudman-Hollings targets for deficit reduction will impose fiscal restraint severe enough to end the expansion and bring on recession. The near-term outlook just

Table 2-3. *Actual and Structural Budget Deficit (−) Targets,*
Fiscal Years 1985–91
Percent of GNP

Year	Actual[a]	Structural[b]	Change in structural surplus from 1986
1985	−5.3	−4.0	. . .
1986	−4.8	−3.9	. . .
1987	−3.1	−2.5	1.4
1988	−2.2	−1.9	2.0
1989	−1.3	−1.3	2.6
1990	−0.6	−0.6	3.3
1991	0	0	3.9

Source: Authors' estimates.
a. Based on Gramm-Rudman-Hollings targets for the unified budget deficit and actual real GNP growth of 3.5 percent a year.
b. Based on a trend real GNP growth rate of 2.5 percent a year at 5.5 percent unemployment. (For a discussion of these assumptions, see the appendix to this chapter.)

discussed suggests this is not likely in the immediate future. What are the prospects for 1987–89, when most of the deficit cutting is scheduled to take place and the economy's near-term strength will no longer be relevant?

The path of reduction in the deficit called for in the legislation is indeed steep. The actual budget deficit is expected to be about 4.8 percent of GNP in 1986 and is to fall to 1.3 percent by 1989 (see table 2-3). Some of the projected reduction in the actual deficit, however, is a result of the expected improvement in the economy. There is a more gradual reduction in the structural deficit, which is a better measure of the restrictive effect on the economy.[2] The reduction in fiscal stimulus of 1.4 percentage points of GNP in 1987 is still large by past standards, although fiscal shifts of 1 percent of GNP in a year have been made in the past. The sustained shift of 2.6 percent of GNP over the three years from 1987 to 1989 is further from historical precedent, except perhaps for the period immediately after World War II. However, this unusual fiscal shift cannot be viewed in isolation. What happens to the exchange rate and trade balance, where

2. The appendix to this chapter discusses the construction of this series for the high-employment structural deficit.

comparably large shifts may occur, will make a major difference in how the economy adjusts to lower budget deficits.

Adjustment and the Exchange Rate

A shift in the exchange rate can have an effect on the aggregate economy that is similar to a shift in fiscal policy, although with different time lags. It alters the trade balance that will accompany any specified levels of GNP here and abroad. A lower exchange rate can therefore stimulate the economy, as would a more expansionary budget; and a higher exchange rate can restrain it, as would a more restrictive budget. The rate of growth in foreign economies has a similar effect, shifting the U.S. trade balance at any given level of U.S. demand.

The importance of a continued fall in the dollar as an offset to reductions in the budget deficit is illustrated by the calculations in table 2-4. Those calculations suggest that if the dollar were to remain unchanged at the level prevailing at the beginning of 1986, the current account deficit would continue to rise slightly and would still be about 3 percent of GNP by 1989. However, if the dollar were to fall in value by 15 percent a year during 1986–88, the current account deficit would fall from 2.8 percent of GNP in 1986 to only 0.5 percent by 1989 and would reach a surplus in 1990. By that time, the difference between the two projections of the current account is close to the size of the budget deficit reductions along the target path (see the last columns of tables 2-3 and 2-4). If a current account path similar to the declining exchange rate projection materialized, it would greatly help in the adjustment to the budget targets.[3]

At present, the policies most likely to produce a further decline in the dollar include tighter budgets in the United States, easier budgets in most countries abroad, and a narrowing of interest rate differentials between the United States and major foreign coun-

3. When preparing the calculations underlying table 2-4 and the related calculations in tables 2-6 and 2-8, we have used a forecasting model for current account transactions developed by William L. Helkie and Lois Stekler. A description of the trade and price equations is available in Helkie, "A Forecasting Model for the U.S. Merchandise Trade Balance," paper prepared for the Fifth Annual Symposium on Forecasting, Montreal, June 1985. We are grateful to Helkie for his assistance in the calculations, but he is not responsible for the inferences we have drawn from them.

Table 2-4. *Projected Current Account Balance with Alternative Paths for the Dollar's Exchange Value, 1985–90*[a]
Billions of dollars unless otherwise indicated

Year	Unchanged exchange rate[b]		Declining exchange rate[c]		Difference	
	Level	Percent of GNP	Level	Percent of GNP	Level	Percent of GNP
1985	− 115	− 2.9	− 115	− 2.9	. . .	. . .
1986	− 134	− 2.9	− 131	− 2.8	3	0.1
1987	− 127	− 2.5	− 105	− 2.0	22	0.5
1988	− 148	− 2.9	− 73	− 1.4	75	1.5
1989	− 165	− 3.0	− 25	− 0.5	140	2.5
1990	− 185	− 3.2	12	0.1	197	3.3

Source: Authors' calculations based on a forecasting model for current account transactions developed by William L. Helkie and Lois Stekler (see note 3).

a. Assumes real GNP growth of 3.5 percent a year for United States and major foreign countries.

b. Assumes weighted-average exchange value of the dollar to be fixed at the level prevailing at the beginning of 1986.

c. Assumes weighted-average exchange value for the dollar to decline at a 15 percent annual rate during 1986–88 and to stabilize thereafter at a rate 10 percent below the 1980 level.

tries, particularly for long-term rates. Since September 1985 the dollar's decline has been aided by the announcements and currency interventions of other governments. If these governments could agree on the desirability of a still lower dollar, they could help bring it about through an appropriate mix of their policies and, if needed, a continuation of the September 1985 approach to intervention in the exchange market.

Much as it would help the U.S. economy adjust to lower budget deficits, a declining dollar has other effects that could cause policymakers either here or abroad to resist it. To be effective in improving the trade balance, a falling dollar must raise the relative price of foreign goods. This would raise the U.S. price level, adding to the annual inflation rate for a time, and to some degree ratcheting up the ongoing inflation rate. The U.S. monetary authorities would not welcome the added price pressures; to avoid them, the authorities might resist a dollar decline that they believed was too large or too rapid.

Improved competitiveness for U.S. industries means reduced

Table 2-5. *Measures of the Underlying Inflation Rate in the United States, 1980–85*
Annual percent change

Index	1980:4	1981:4	1982:4	1983:4	1984:4	1985:4
CPI less food, energy, shelter, and used cars	9.6	8.7	6.1	4.1	4.2	4.1
PCE deflator less food and energy[a]	9.7	8.8	6.4	4.4	4.4	4.2
PPI less food and energy	10.8	7.6	4.9	2.1	2.2	2.7
Average hourly earnings index[b]	9.6	8.4	6.0	3.9	3.0	3.2
Employment cost index[c]	9.7	9.8	6.4	5.7	4.9	3.9

Sources: Department of Commerce, Bureau of Economic Analysis, *Survey of Current Business,* various issues; *Economic Report of the President,* various years; and data from U.S. Department of Labor, Bureau of Labor Statistics.
a. PCE is the GNP deflator for personal consumption expenditures.
b. Earnings of production workers.
c. Average hourly compensation of all private workers.

competitiveness for their foreign counterparts. Foreign policy-makers might therefore resist a further dollar decline, either to avoid the structural shifts the loss of competitiveness would entail within their own economies or simply to respond to political pressures from their own affected industries.

The inflation rate in the United States has been slowing steadily since the deep recession of the early 1980s. Table 2-5 summarizes several indicators of the underlying inflation rate that ought to be the main concern of policymakers. These indicators remove the direct effects of volatile prices, such as those for food and fuel, from standard indexes in order to gauge progress in the stubborn inflation trend that is closely related to wage costs and productivity, at least in the United States. The indicators based on price indexes show a leveling off of inflation at a modest rate since 1983. The employment cost index, which is the most comprehensive and accurate indicator of hourly labor costs, continued to drop through 1985.

Because underlying inflation trends change slowly, inflation should not reemerge as a serious problem unless markets are

Table 2-6. *Total Stimulus Associated with Achievement of Budget Targets and Alternative Exchange Rates and Foreign Growth Rates, Fiscal Years 1985–91*[a]
Percent of GNP

Year	Fiscal stimulus[b]	Foreign stimulus[c]	Net combined stimulus
Case A			
Dollar declines 15 percent a year during 1986–88;			
3.5 percent foreign growth rate			
1985	4.0	−3.6	0.4
1986	3.9	−3.4	0.5
1987	2.5	−2.4	0.1
1988	1.9	−1.6	0.3
1989	1.3	−0.5	0.8
1990	0.6	0.1	0.7
1991	0	0.1	0.1
Case B			
Dollar declines 15 percent a year during 1986–88;			
2.5 percent foreign growth rate			
1985	4.0	−3.6	0.4
1986	3.9	−3.5	0.4
1987	2.5	−2.8	−0.3
1988	1.9	−2.3	−0.4
1989	1.3	−1.6	−0.3
1990	0.6	−1.4	−0.8
1991	0	−1.4	−1.4
Case C			
Dollar remains at level of January 1, 1986;			
3.5 percent foreign growth rate			
1985	4.0	−3.6	0.4
1986	3.9	−3.8	0.1
1987	2.5	−3.3	−0.8
1988	1.9	−3.7	−1.8
1989	1.3	−3.5	−2.2
1990	0.6	−3.5	−2.9
1991	0	−3.5	−3.5

allowed to become overly tight, as they were in the last half of the 1960s. At high employment, the trend of inflation can be expected to be a little above the underlying inflation rates of 1985. In the immediate future, lower oil prices will produce actual inflation rates below the trend. Afterward, actual inflation rates will exceed

Table 2-6 *(continued)*

Year	Fiscal stimulus[b]	Foreign stimulus[c]	Net combined stimulus
Case D			
Dollar remains at level of January 1, 1986;			
2.5 percent foreign growth rate			
1985	4.0	−3.6	0.4
1986	3.9	−3.9	0
1987	2.5	−3.7	−1.2
1988	1.9	−4.4	−2.5
1989	1.3	−4.6	−3.3
1990	0.6	−5.0	−4.4
1991	0	−5.0	−5.0

Addendum

Case	GNP price deflator[d]	Consumer price index[d]	Treasury bill rate[d,e]
Case A	4.3	5.4	6.9
Case B	4.2	5.3	6.0
Case C	3.7	3.8	4.6
Case D	3.6	3.7	3.9

Sources: Simulations of U.S. international transactions underlying calculations of foreign stimulus make use of forecasting model developed by Helkie and Stekler (see note 3). Adjustments of foreign stimulus to a high-employment basis and figures for inflation rates and interest rates are rough estimates made by authors.

a. All cases assume economic activity in United States expands at 3.5 percent a year.
b. Structural deficit (see table 2-3) with sign reversed.
c. Current account balance at high employment.
d. Averages for 1987–89, percent a year.
e. Three-month.

the trend if the dollar continues to depreciate; that outcome will be the inevitable unwinding of the favorable price effects experienced when the dollar was rising in value. We do not believe these inflation prospects should deter policymakers from pursuing a further decline in the dollar to more competitive levels that would actually eliminate the current account deficit.

Alternative Adjustment Paths

Table 2-6 illustrates the effect on the economy of meeting the high-employment budget targets shown in table 2-3 under four alternative scenarios for the dollar exchange rate and foreign growth rates. The table presents both the fiscal stimulus (the structural deficit with the sign reversed) and the foreign stimulus (the current account balance adjusted to a high-employment basis) as percentages of each year's GNP. The sum of the two approximates the net expansionary or contractionary stimulus from these sources. Between 1980 and 1985 that sum actually declined slightly as the swing to a current account deficit slightly outweighed the growing structural deficit in the budget.

For each of the scenarios shown in table 2-6, it is assumed that economic activity in the United States expands at a steady rate of 3.5 percent a year. The implicit presumption is that monetary policy produces the variations in U.S. interest rates needed to keep the economy on the desired path of expansion in the face of the changes in fiscal and external stimuli. An addendum to the table indicates rough estimates of the average Treasury bill rate during 1987–89 that might be consistent with maintaining the steady expansion in each scenario. It also provides estimates of the average inflation rates for each case.

Case A is among the more likely outcomes and would pose only modest risks of economic instability. It assumes that meeting the budget targets would be accompanied by foreign growth at an annual rate of 3.5 percent and a steady 15 percent annual depreciation of the dollar during 1986–88. This foreign growth rate is more than 1 percentage point faster than the average for European countries in the past two years. Their growth was still slower before that. The combination of buoyant growth abroad and a declining dollar would bring the U.S. current account into balance by 1990. The total stimulus from fiscal and foreign sources would not change much in this case, and short-term interest rates on Treasury bills would average very near their level in early 1986. The inevitable drawback would be a somewhat faster rise in consumer prices than that experienced during the past three years.

In case B the dollar is assumed to follow the same declining path, but the foreign GNP growth rate is only 2.5 percent. As a result, the improvement in the current account would be substantially smaller. At 1.6 percent of GNP, the current account deficit would still be $85 billion in 1989. There would be a noticeable drop in the combined stimulus in 1987, and interest rates would average about 1 percentage point less than in the previous case. The adjustment to declining budget deficits in this case still does not appear difficult. We think foreign economies will expand faster than 2.5 percent in the near future, so this case seems less likely than case A.

In the last two cases shown in the table, the dollar is assumed to remain unchanged from its level at the beginning of 1986. In these scenarios, the combined stimulus to the economy would be steadily reduced. Inflation would average less than 4 percent and interest rates would have to decline substantially to maintain 3.5 percent growth in the U.S. economy. In case D, which combines slower growth abroad with an unchanged dollar, the total restraint on the economy would be so severe that it might not be possible for monetary policy to offset it. The estimated Treasury bill rate would be virtually the same as the increase in the GNP price deflator, but that might not be low enough to avoid recession. Case D is not among the most likely outcomes. Indeed, by early March 1986 the dollar had already fallen 7 percent below the value assumed for cases C and D. These calculations nonetheless illustrate the importance of a declining dollar and vigorous foreign growth in aiding the adjustment to lower U.S. budget deficits.

Failure to Meet Budget Targets

If the Gramm-Rudman-Hollings budget targets are not adhered to because of a political stalemate over how to achieve them, a different range of outcomes would be relevant. At this point, nobody expects the structural deficit to continue rising as a share of GNP. But to characterize the kind of outcome a political stalemate could produce, we project a budget path somewhat above the Congressional Budget Office's baseline projection (see table 2-7). This includes a 3 percent growth rate for real defense spending, rather than the zero growth assumed in the CBO baseline, and nondefense spending higher than the baseline by the same dollar amounts as this difference in defense spending. This stalemate deficit path keeps the dollar value of deficits little changed. As a share of GNP, the deficit declines a little in 1987 and only slightly thereafter.

Table 2-7. *Budget Deficits with Political Stalemate,*
Fiscal Years 1986–91
Billions of dollars unless otherwise indicated

Item	1986	1987	1988	1989	1990	1991
CBO baseline of						
February 1986	− 208	− 181	− 165	− 144	− 120	− 104
Adjusted for 3 percent						
defense growth	. . .	− 184	− 175	− 162	− 148	− 144
Stalemate deficit[a]	. . .	− 187	− 185	− 180	− 176	− 184
Stalemate deficit as						
percent of GNP	− 3.9	− 3.5	− 3.4	− 3.3	− 3.0	− 2.9
Addendum						
Target deficit as						
percent of GNP	− 4.8	− 3.1	− 2.2	− 1.3	− 0.6	0

Sources: Congressional Budget Office, *The Economic and Budget Outlook: Fiscal Years 1987–1991* (GPO, 1986), p. 69; and authors' estimates.

a. Previous row increased each year by the same dollar amount as the difference between the CBO baseline for defense spending and defense spending at a 3 percent growth rate.

Table 2-8 presents two additional scenarios to illustrate the impact of a stalemate deficit in conjunction with the alternative exchange rate assumptions used in table 2-6. Both of the stalemate outcomes would present serious problems, and neither is likely to be sustainable indefinitely.

In case E, because the exchange rate is assumed to remain at the level of the beginning of 1986, the foreign stimulus would not change much. With little reduction in the budget deficit, the combined stimulus would be virtually constant from 1985 on. This outcome would pose few stabilization problems, at least initially. Interest rates in 1987–89 might average a little higher than their recent levels. But this outcome would not solve the long-term problems inherent in both the budget and trade deficits and for that reason would probably be unstable. Although the economy could continue to expand with the twin deficits for a time, it is unlikely that the large current account deficits and corresponding inflows of foreign funds could continue throughout 1987–89 with an unchanged exchange rate.

Case F combines the assumptions of a stalemate on the budget and a sustained, steady depreciation of the dollar. This scenario

Table 2-8. *Total Stimulus Associated with Stalemate on Budget
Deficit and Alternative Exchange Rates and Foreign Growth Rates,
Fiscal Years 1985–91*[a]
Percent of GNP

Year	Fiscal stimulus[b]	Foreign stimulus[c]	Net combined stimulus
Case E			
Dollar remains at level of January 1, 1986;			
3.5 percent foreign growth rate			
1985	4.0	−3.6	0.4
1986	3.9	−3.5	0.4
1987	3.5	−2.9	0.6
1988	3.4	−3.1	0.3
1989	3.3	−3.0	0.3
1990	3.0	−3.2	0.2
1991	2.9	−3.2	−0.3
Case F			
Dollar declines 15 percent a year during 1986–88;			
3.5 percent foreign growth rate			
1985	4.0	−3.6	0.4
1986	3.9	−3.4	0.5
1987	3.5	−2.4	1.1
1988	3.4	−1.6	1.8
1989	3.3	−0.5	2.8
1990	3.0	0.1	3.1
1991	2.9	0.1	3.0

Addendum

Case	GNP price deflator[d]	Consumer price index[d]	Treasury bill rate[d,e]
Case E	3.7	3.8	7.5
Case F	4.3	5.4	10.0

Source: See table 2-6.
a. Both cases assume economic activity in the United States expands at 3.5 percent a year.
b. Structural deficit (see table 2-3) with sign reversed.
c. Current account balance at high employment.
d. Averages for 1987–89, percent a year.
e. Three-month.

would gradually eliminate the current account deficit. With the structural budget deficit remaining high, however, the combined stimulus from fiscal and foreign sources would grow rapidly. Other things being equal, interest rates would have to rise sharply to squeeze out domestic investment and keep the economy from overheating. Case F would probably also be unstable. Indeed, rather than declining smoothly, the dollar could fall precipitously and disruptively. Disappointment about the prospects for reducing the U.S. budget deficit might even lead participants in financial markets to push the dollar down so far as to substantially overshoot the level consistent with longer-run balance in U.S. international transactions. Such disorder in exchange markets, especially if combined with the sharp falls and greater volatility in domestic stock and bond prices that might accompany sharply higher interest rates, would cause acute uncertainty in the Federal Reserve about the proper conduct of monetary policy and would raise the likelihood of recession. Of all the outcomes considered here, a political stalemate over the budget deficit, together with a rapid decline in the dollar, poses the gravest risks for the U.S. economy.

Should the Budget Be Balanced by 1991?

Thus far we have argued that the economy would benefit from substantially lower federal deficits and that the Gramm-Rudman-Hollings targets through 1989 can probably be achieved without slowing economic growth, provided monetary authorities are accommodative and the value of the dollar comes down substantially. But should the country aim for a *balanced* budget by 1991?

Whether the deficit under high-employment conditions should be cut to, say, 1 percent of GNP or entirely eliminated is a controversial question; the answer is much less certain than the response to the broader proposition that the deficit ought to be reduced very sharply during 1986–89. To set an appropriate target for the longer run, one must consider both the effects of the federal budget on the *level* of aggregate demand and GNP and its consequences for the *structure* of GNP. A lower structural deficit (higher surplus) increases net national saving and allows room for higher levels of investment. If lower interest rates or other

Table 2-9. *Domestic Investment Needed at High Employment,*
1955–79, 1984–85, and 1991
Percent of GNP

Period or year	High-employment federal surplus	+	Other national saving[a]	=	High-employment net national saving	−	High-employment net foreign investment	=	Needed net domestic investment at high employment
Earlier high-employment periods									
1955–57	1.3		7.2		8.5		0.5		8.0
1964–66	−0.3		8.9		8.6		0.8		7.8
1972–73	−1.4		9.6		8.2		0.8		7.4
1977–79	−1.3		8.9		7.6		−0.3		7.9
Recent past									
1984–85	−3.7		8.5		4.8		−3.5		8.3
Projected 1991									
Historical current account balance	0		8.5		8.5		0.1		8.4
Recent current account balance	0		8.5		8.5		−3.5		12.0

Sources: Department of Commerce, Bureau of Economic Analysis, *Survey of Current Business,* various issues; and authors' estimates.

a. State and local government surplus plus net private saving. The statistical discrepancy in the national income accounts is assumed to be zero.

conditions generate a corresponding increase in demand for investment goods, they will be produced and the desired level of total GNP will be maintained, with investment as a larger share of the total.

But generating more national saving will not automatically call forth sufficient investment demand. There may be limits to how much investment can be stimulated by lower interest rates. If national saving exceeds the total investment that would be forthcoming at high employment, total demand will be insufficient to achieve high employment. The historical record can offer guidance on what level of structural surplus or deficit has been consistent with high employment in the past.

Table 2-9 adapts the analysis of saving and investment flows from table 2-1 to investigate the level of investment demand needed to support high employment and a balanced budget for 1991. The federal surplus and net foreign investment, which are both sensitive to departures of the economy from high employment, are shown at their high-employment (structural) levels. The table adds high-employment federal surpluses or deficits and other national saving and subtracts high-employment net foreign investment to arrive at the domestic investment needed to maintain the economy at high employment.

The first column of table 2-9 shows that maintaining a balanced budget represents a somewhat more restrictive fiscal policy than was typical of most prior periods of high employment, except the mid-1950s. Indeed, the deficit of 1.3 percent anticipated for 1989 under the target path (table 2-3) is close to the average experience in the other periods shown here. Therefore a simple historical comparison might suggest that a deficit ratio of about that size is an appropriate goal. But the other elements of saving and investment must also be taken into account.

The remaining columns of table 2-9 show that the 8.5 percent ratio of other national saving in 1984–85 was in the middle of the experience of past high-employment periods. But the − 3.5 percent net foreign investment ratio of 1984–85 is well outside previous experience. How that evolves in the future will make a big difference to the appropriate level of the deficit. The two 1991 projections in the table illustrate this point.

For the 1991 projections we assume the total of private saving at high employment and state and local surpluses remains at the recent level of 8.5 percent of GNP. If net foreign investment were to return to its historical average of 0.1 percent of GNP, domestic investment would then have to total 8.4 percent of GNP to maintain high employment with a balanced federal budget. Net domestic investment has been above 8 percent of GNP in five of the past thirty years, all of them years of high employment and high capacity utilization—1955, 1965, 1966, 1973, and 1978. It has averaged 8 percent of GNP over the following longer intervals: 1955–56, 1964–69, 1972–73, and 1977–79. These thirteen years are generally thought of as periods of high or over-full employment. These comparisons suggest that maintaining the investment share of GNP above 8 percent would be unusual but probably not out of reach if the economy remained around its high-employment level and interest rates were kept very low.

In sharp contrast, if high-employment net foreign investment were to remain at its recent level of − 3.5 percent of GNP, the domestic investment needed to maintain high employment in the face of a balanced budget would be 12 percent of GNP, as the last row of table 2-9 shows. That ratio is totally outside the range of experience, and it is implausible that it could be achieved regardless of the monetary policy pursued.

To summarize, if net foreign investment returned to its historical average—implying a positive swing of nearly 4 percent of GNP in the current account balance—and if private investment, spurred by low interest rates and an appropriately accommodative monetary policy, rose to match the increase in available saving, a balanced-budget policy would be consistent with maintaining high employment. And simultaneously it would make possible a shift in the structure of the U.S. economy toward greater investment. Given the very low rate of productivity growth in the United States during recent years, this structural change would be desirable.[4]

On the other hand, if private investment demand, even with relatively low interest rates, should fail to rise sufficiently to match the expanded flow of available saving, or if the current account remained in substantial deficit with a continued large inflow of saving from abroad, total demand for goods and services in the economy would be too weak to sustain high employment. Production would tend to sag and unemployment would rise. In that event a balanced-budget policy would be inconsistent with high employment.

This far in advance of events it is difficult to make a firm judgment about whether a balanced budget in 1991 (and presumably beyond) is sound policy. But there is no need to make such a judgment now. Policies to start reducing present deficits are clearly desirable. Economic developments in the next three years, as the

4. Some would go further and argue that proper economic policy should aim for an overall *surplus* in the federal budget during coming decades. Starting in the second decade of the next century, the fraction of the U.S. population drawing social security benefits will rise sharply. To avoid a major drain on the incomes of future working generations because of higher payroll taxes, it is argued, the country should begin now to run a large surplus in the social security trust fund and indirectly use that surplus to finance an increase in the nation's stock of productive capital. In that way the sharply higher social security benefits of the next century can be matched by higher national output and income. Such a policy would require that the overall budget be in surplus by an amount at least equal to the surplus in the social security trust funds. The big question, however, is whether the existence of a large budget surplus and plentiful national savings would itself induce an equal increase in private investment. Unless that happened, the budget surplus would lead not to higher investment but to a weak economy and low GNP.

country pursues deficit reductions, will help determine whether
aiming ultimately for a balanced budget is sound policy.

The Problem with Fixed Budget Targets

We have thus far considered two important issues concerning
deficit reduction: whether it is wise to aim for cuts on the rapid
Gramm-Rudman-Hollings schedule, and whether it is desirable to
aim eventually for a balanced budget. Quite apart from whether
the Gramm-Rudman-Hollings targets are appropriate general goals,
we must consider whether it is desirable to bind policy to them
regardless of future economic conditions.

Before passage of the Gramm-Rudman-Hollings legislation, the
federal budget acted as an automatic stabilizer for the economy.
As the economy varied cyclically, the actual deficit deviated from
the structural deficit, cushioning a weakening of the economy and
exerting restraint during times of vigorous growth. In addition,
policymakers in the past could change the structural deficit by
making additional discretionary changes in expenditures or taxes
to help offset major departures of the economy from its desired
path.

Fixed targets for the actual deficit preclude both automatic and
discretionary changes in the budget to cushion economic fluctua-
tions. Still worse, they require spending cuts or tax increases if
economic activity slows. Such actions would aggravate a slowdown. Thus the fixed targets of Gramm-Rudman-Hollings could
turn out to have perverse economic effects during recession or
sustained slow growth.

The new law tries to solve this problem with an escape clause,
but that clause has an important flaw. The legislation provides
that if actual economic growth is below 1 percent for two consec-
utive quarters, or if the director of the CBO forecasts a two-
quarter decline in real GNP any time in the year ahead, Congress
can suspend the law under expedited procedures. However, only
the rate of change in GNP, not its level, is taken into account in
determining whether this clause can be invoked. At the start of a
recession or a period of slow growth, the conditions would be met
and it would be easy to postpone the deficit targets. But in most
postwar American recessions, although the economy has begun

Table 2-10. *Estimated Baseline Deficits under Weak-Economy Assumption Compared with Gramm-Rudman-Hollings Targets, Fiscal Years 1987–91*
Billions of dollars

Year	Baseline with weak economy[a]	Gramm-Rudman-Hollings target	Required cuts from baseline
1987	224	144	80
1988	282	108	174
1989	271	72	199
1990	238	36	202
1991	237	0	237

Source: CBO, *The Economic and Budget Outlook: Fiscal Years 1987–1991*, pp. xiv, 70.
    a. Assumes recession similar to the 1973–75 recession starting in 1987.

to recover about a year after the trough, unemployment has remained high, revenues depressed, and the deficit abnormally large. In such circumstances, the legal conditions for a waiver would not be met, and massive cuts in government spending would be required to meet the now-reinstated deficit targets.

Table 2-10 illustrates what could happen if a moderately severe recession began in the first quarter of 1987. Deficits would balloon as unemployment insurance and other countercyclical expenditures rose and tax collections fell below projections. The first column shows what the CBO baseline deficits would become under these economic developments. The Gramm-Rudman-Hollings targets would be waived for 1988, but not for 1989 and later. The implied deficit cut from the baseline for 1989 would equal almost $200 billion, but attempts to cut spending or raise taxes by this magnitude would drastically reduce chances for economic recovery. Even a very expansive Federal Reserve policy would have difficulties offsetting such fiscal measures. Recovery could be postponed, if not aborted.

In this example, when the CBO economists made their economic forecast for 1989, they would have to assume a budget that incorporated large cuts in spending or increases in tax rates. This assumption would necessarily lower their estimates of GNP and the tax base, producing the need for still larger spending cuts or tax rate increases to meet the target. The outcome would be similar and also undesirable if the target had to be met when annual economic growth was below the rate needed to keep unemployment from rising—perhaps 2.5 percent a year at present—but above the 1 percent needed to trigger the waiver.

Policy Conclusions

This analysis points inexorably to the conclusion that budget deficits should be reduced from their present levels toward levels more compatible with historical experience. Specifying a rigid target path for those reductions, however, is potentially harmful. If a target path is deemed necessary for political reasons, budget targets should be expressed in terms of structural rather than actual deficits to avoid a perverse effect on economic stability if the economy falters.

Apart from its symbolic value, a balanced budget has no special relevance. The nation should postpone decisions on whether a balanced budget should be the ultimate goal for 1991. For now it is impossible to say whether that target would be compatible with maintaining high employment.

The evolution of the nation's current account balance will be as important to macroeconomic performance as the shift in the budget deficit. Reducing the present deficit in the current account will help the economic transition to lower structural budget deficits. And restoring balance or even a surplus in the current account in the future would permit a lower federal budget deficit, or even balance or a surplus.

The two main determinants of the current account balance are relative growth rates here and abroad and the dollar's exchange value. Between 1981 and 1985 the fiscal policy of the United States differed dramatically from that of Germany and Japan, leading to both differential growth rates and a massive appreciation of the dollar that together produced large swings in each country's current account balance (see table 2-11).

Growth in Europe has been inadequate throughout the 1980s, leading to increases in unemployment every year. Growth has been better in Japan, but has depended heavily on exports rather than on domestic demand. Stimulating domestic demand in both Europe and Japan would help to solve their own problems as well

Table 2-11. *Change in Structural Budget Surplus and Current Account Balance, United States, Japan, and Germany, 1981–85*
Percent of GNP

Country	Change in structural budget surplus	Change in current account balance
United States	−2.9	−3.0
Japan	2.2	3.3
Germany	3.5	2.9

Sources: OECD, *Economic Outlook*, vol. 36 (December 1985); and Department of Commerce, Bureau of Economic Analysis, *Survey of Current Business*, various issues.

as mesh perfectly with reducing fiscal stimulus in the United States.

Changes in fiscal and monetary policies here and abroad should be accompanied by enough reduction in the dollar's exchange value to bring current account balances back toward historical norms. There is resistance to further depreciation of the dollar because of its effects on inflation in the United States and on export industries abroad. This resistance is misguided, however. So long as the dollar must eventually depreciate further, the side effects of its decline can be delayed but not avoided. And in view of other developments in the U.S. and foreign economies, the present is probably as good a time as any to absorb the price and output effects of dollar depreciation.

Interest rates will have to adjust to keep the U.S. and foreign economies growing smoothly in coming years. The range of U.S. interest rates that could be required under alternative paths for the budget deficit and current account is very wide (tables 2-6 and 2-8). And monetary aggregates have proven to be unreliable as the primary focus for the conduct of policy. It is thus impossible to specify in advance a detailed blueprint for future monetary policy, and inappropriate to try to do so. Instead, the Federal Reserve will have to adjust bank reserves and interest rates in response to emerging economic conditions, as it has been doing for the past few years.

A difficult stabilization problem for the Federal Reserve could arise if major surprises occur in budgetary policies or elsewhere. The economy does not respond immediately to changes in monetary policy. If the Gramm-Rudman-Hollings cuts in the structural budget deficit are going to be made in the fall of 1986, they can be accommodated most easily if the Federal Reserve and financial markets have anticipated them well in advance. That is what markets appear to have done in recent months. But the threat of political stalemate in coming months could unsettle those markets, reverse some of the favorable movements in bond prices and exchange rates, and hamper the transition to large budget cuts if they eventually are made. Therefore a prompt settlement of the differences between the president and Congress over how to reduce deficits would be very useful because it would reduce uncertainty.

Appendix

Estimates of the structural deficits implicit in the Gramm-Rudman-Hollings targets are helpful in assessing their likely economic impact. To construct such estimates, it is first necessary to decide on a suitable high-employment path along which to calculate the budget deficits. Although the aggregate unemployment rate is the most commonly used proxy for an aggregate utilization rate, it has drifted relative to other indicators because of demographic and other changes in the economy. The same overall tightness of markets that used to correspond to a 4 or 5 percent unemployment rate in earlier decades apparently came to correspond to a 6 percent unemployment rate in the 1970s.

Table 2-12 shows three measures of unemployment for recent years and intervals: the aggregate unemployment rate, a demographically weighted unemployment rate, and the unemployment rate for males aged 20–64. The difference between the aggregate rate and the two other measures has recently narrowed after widening for much of the period. Since either the weighted or the adult male unemployment rate is a more accurate proxy for the tightness in labor markets than the aggregate rate, this indicates that the average market conditions that prevailed at 6 percent unemployment during the 1970s and until recently would be associated with a somewhat lower unemployment rate now and in the years ahead.

Table 2-12. *Aggregate and Alternative Unemployment Rates,*
1954–85
Percent

Period or year	Unemployment rate measure			Differences	
	Aggregate	Weighted	Adult males[a]	Aggregate less weighted	Aggregate less adult male
1954–59	5.1	4.3	4.4	0.8	0.7
1960–69	4.8	3.6	3.6	1.2	1.2
1970–79	6.2	4.5	4.5	1.7	1.7
1980	7.1	5.7	5.9	1.4	1.2
1981	7.6	5.9	6.3	1.7	1.3
1982	9.7	8.3	8.8	1.4	0.9
1983	9.6	8.4	8.9	1.2	0.7
1984	7.5	6.4	6.6	1.1	0.9
1985	7.2	6.1	6.2	1.1	1.0

Sources: Data from Department of Labor, Bureau of Labor Statistics; and authors'
estimates of demographically weighted unemployment rate.
  a. Males aged 20–64.

Based on the present relationship among the three rates, a 5.5
percent aggregate rate would correspond to about a 4.5 percent
rate for either of the other measures. Since markets have not in
the past been overly tight with a 4.5 percent weighted or adult
male rate, we can choose a 5.5 percent aggregate unemployment
rate as the benchmark for calculating structural deficits in 1985–
90. For earlier years, the aggregate unemployment benchmark
rises from 4.5 in the 1950s and 1960s to 6 percent in the last half of
the 1970s.

The level and growth rate of GNP along this benchmark path,
known as potential GNP, is the next necessary ingredient for
estimating structural deficits. Productivity growth has continued
to be disappointing, so potential GNP has not been growing rapidly
despite the rapid growth of the labor force in recent years.
Measuring over periods with similar unemployment rates, so as
to minimize the effects of rising or falling unemployment on
growth, we find trend GNP in recent years grew at an average rate
of 2.7 percent between 1976–77 and 1980–81 and 2.3 percent
between 1980–81 and 1984–85. Allowing for some productivity

improvement as the work force continues to mature and a lower dollar shifts output toward high-productivity manufacturing industries, we can assume a 2.5 percent annual growth in potential output between 1985 and 1990, the same as over the longer interval from 1976–77 to 1984–85. Based on historical relations between unemployment rates and output gaps (the percentage by which GNP falls below or above potential), a 3.5 percent annual growth rate in real GNP would bring GNP up to potential in 1990 with the aggregate unemployment rate at 5.5 percent.

3

Budgetary Options

IN THIS CHAPTER we explore three alternative budget strategies—
each with a different view of the desirable level and mix of federal
activities—for reaching the deficit targets in fiscal years 1987–89.
First, we analyze what we think would be the disastrous consequences for future federal budgets of implementing the automatic
budget-cutting procedures of the Gramm-Rudman-Hollings law
for fiscal 1987–89. We also outline a less extreme version of this
alternative, in which Congress would preserve the broad budget
priorities of the new law but avoid the automatic cuts.

Second, we discuss the implications of the administration's
budget strategy, which eschews tax increases, continues defense
spending growth, and cuts domestic spending drastically.

Finally, we offer our own preferred budget strategy, which
would allow somewhat more defense spending than the Gramm-
Rudman-Hollings alternative and cut less than either of the others
out of domestic spending, but would make a small reduction in
social security benefits and require a tax increase.

While the three strategies would have slightly different effects
on the economy as a whole, these differences are hard to predict
and not likely to be large. The choice among them is mainly a
matter of budgetary priorities: what level and mix of services do
Americans want from government, given the need to pay for them
with more taxes and less borrowing than at present?

Although we provide estimates of the budgetary consequences
of the three alternative strategies for fiscal 1987, our emphasis is
on longer-term consequences, for which we use the budget in
fiscal 1989 as a symbol. It might be possible, through modest and

51

partly temporary revenue increases and spending cuts coupled with sales of government-owned assets, to pare the 1987 deficit enough to avoid triggering automatic budget cuts while leaving the deficit well above the targets for later years.[1] But such a course would not be sufficient to set in motion the long-term economic benefits that flow from deficit reductions. The healthy decline in long-term interest rates in early 1986, for example, stemmed in part from a belief by financial investors that Congress was making lasting improvements in the deficit. Congress—and the nation— should not focus simply on the upcoming budget year, but on the longer-term future.

The Deficit under "Current Policy"

To estimate how much the deficit is likely to have to fall in order to reach the Gramm-Rudman-Hollings targets, it is necessary to start with a baseline projection of what future budget deficits would be if current spending policies and revenue laws were not changed. The latest Congressional Budget Office projection of the baseline deficit, issued in February 1986, surprised many analysts.[2] Previous outside forecasts, while incorporating lower interest rates and the spending cuts made by Congress in the 1985 session, had nevertheless shown the baseline deficit falling not very far below $200 billion. The CBO February report, on the other hand, projected baseline deficits declining from $208 billion in fiscal 1986 to $104 billion by fiscal 1991. The gap between the projected budget deficit and the deficit targets specified by the new law appeared to be much smaller than anticipated.

There are two principal reasons why the new CBO baseline differs from the earlier outside estimates. First, the Gramm-Rudman-Hollings law required that spending cuts for fiscal 1986 be put into effect in March 1986, and the CBO, following its normal procedure, assumed that those cuts would not be restored in future years. Although the new law required a spending reduc-

1. Under the new law, a projection by the Congressional Budget Office and the Office of Management and Budget that the deficit for the coming year is likely to be within $10 billion of the deficit target is enough to avoid triggering the automatic budget-cutting procedure.

2. Congressional Budget Office, *The Economic and Budget Outlook: Fiscal Year 1987–1991* (GPO, 1986).

tion of only $11.7 billion in 1986, those cuts, if not restored, will lower future annual spending by larger amounts, increasing to almost $23 billion by fiscal 1989. The primary reason is that in many federal programs—procurement of military planes and tanks, construction of roads and waste treatment plants, for example—funds appropriated in any one year (called new budget authority) are actually spent gradually over several years as the new equipment or structures are produced and delivered. To cut actual spending in fiscal 1986 by the required $11.7 billion, Congress had to cut budget authority in that year by about twice as much. If the cut in budget authority is assumed to be permanent, therefore, annual spending will ultimately fall much more than $11.7 billion. In addition the decrease in federal borrowing that is made possible by the spending cuts means lower interest payments on the federal debt.

The second reason that the February baseline was lower than previous estimates arises from the CBO assumption that future defense appropriations would grow only enough to compensate for inflation (zero real growth). While this assumption has traditionally been made for domestic appropriations, recent baseline forecasts had assumed higher growth in defense. The CBO projection of August 1985, for example, had assumed that future defense appropriations would grow at 3 percent after inflation, as specified in the congressional budget resolution for fiscal 1986. The consequences for the deficit of lowering the assumed growth rate for the defense budget are modest at first—only about a $4 billion cut in fiscal 1987—but they rapidly become more significant. By 1989, use of the lower assumption reduces the projected deficit $20 billion; by 1991, an estimated $44 billion.[3]

The substantial effects of these two assumptions on baseline budget deficits may be seen in table 3-1. If Gramm-Rudman-Hollings cuts had not been made in fiscal 1986 and defense spending were still assumed to grow at 3 percent after inflation, the baseline deficit of $220 billion in 1986 would decline only modestly to about $176 billion in fiscal 1991 (column A). If the cuts in fiscal 1986 are assumed to be permanent and defense to grow at 3 percent after inflation, the baseline deficit falls more

3. As before, these estimates include the interest saving that results from the lower spending.

Table 3-1. *Changes in Projections of the Baseline Budget Deficit for Fiscal Years 1986–91*
Billions of dollars

Year	Baseline before 1986 GRH cuts (A)	−	1986 GRH cuts[a]	=	Revised baseline (B)	−	Reductions in defense budget to zero real growth[a]	=	CBO February 1986 baseline (C)
1986	220		12		208		0		208
1987	202		18		184		3		181
1988	197		21		176		11		165
1989	187		23		164		20		144
1990	177		26		151		31		120
1991	176		28		148		44		104

Sources: Column C from Congressional Budget Office, *The Economic and Budget Outlook: Fiscal Years 1987–1991* (Government Printing Office, February 1986); other columns are authors' estimates.

a. Includes the reduction in interest payments that would result from the lower deficits.

rapidly, to $148 billion in 1991 (column B). Finally, if, in addition, defense appropriations are assumed to grow only at the inflation rate, the baseline deficit falls much more steeply, to $104 billion in 1991 (column C). The congressional action needed to attain the deficit targets therefore appears to be much less if one uses the latest CBO baseline than it would be under estimates using earlier assumptions (see table 3-2). On the other hand, having already made substantial reductions in civilian programs under the 1986 Gramm-Rudman-Hollings cuts, Congress will find further reductions more difficult. And halting the buildup in the defense budget in the face of strong opposition from the president will itself require a positive decision by Congress.

New Budget-Cutting Procedures

The three political powers involved in budget making, the president and the Republicans and Democrats in Congress, have for the past three years been at loggerheads over how to apportion large deficit reductions among lower defense spending, lower civilian spending, and tax increases. As the maneuvering dragged

Table 3-2. *Spending Cuts or Tax Increases Needed to Meet Gramm-Rudman-Hollings Deficit Targets, Fiscal Years 1987–91*
Billions of dollars

		Spending cuts or tax increases		
Year	Deficit target	From baseline before 1986 GRH cuts[a]	From baseline after 1986 GRH cuts[b]	From February 1986 CBO baseline[c]
1987	144	58	40	37
1988	108	89	68	57
1989	72	115	92	72
1990	36	141	115	84
1991	0	176	148	104

Source: see table 3-1.
a. Column A, table 3-1.
b. Column B, table 3-1.
c. Column C, table 3-1.

on, evidence of the short-run economic costs and the potential long-run damages from massive budget deficits began to mount. Political pressures to "do something about the deficit" became intense. Unable to break the impasse over how to cut the deficit, but unwilling to accept any longer the political costs of inaction, the three political power centers collaborated during the closing days of last year to adopt the unique legislative approach embodied in Gramm-Rudman-Hollings.

The law sets annual deficit targets that take the budget deficit to zero during the next five years. If in any year the parties to the dispute cannot reach agreement on the specific measures needed to achieve those targets, the law provides a mechanical sequestration formula that cuts budget authority for defense and civilian spending in approximately equal amounts sufficient in combination to achieve that goal.[4]

All of the participants in the dispute—the president and most members of both parties in Congress—agree that blind application of the mechanical formula for spending reductions would play havoc with national security and the civilian operations of the

4. If its procedures are triggered, the new law takes back from government agencies some of the budget authority that has earlier been provided. That process was given the name "sequestration."

federal government. The law, therefore, is seen by most of those who voted for it as a "doomsday machine": its consequences are so awful that contemplation of them is assumed to compel the disputing parties to come to agreement. Not surprisingly, however, each of the parties believes that it will be the others who will capitulate. Thus President Reagan, who is strongly opposed both to a tax increase and to eliminating defense growth, supports the bill on the assumption that it will force Congress to cut civilian spending. Many congressional supporters of the law in both political parties believe that it will finally force the president to agree to a tax increase rather than preside over a large slash in defense spending. A smaller number of congressional supporters believe it will sharply reverse the buildup in the defense budget.

In early February the three-judge U.S. District Court for the District of Columbia unanimously declared unconstitutional a central feature of the new law—namely the delegation to the comptroller general of responsibility for validating and forwarding to the president the CBO and OMB estimates of how much each program must be cut. The case is being appealed to the Supreme Court. In the interim the 1986 cuts already being applied to federal spending programs will continue in force.

If the Supreme Court should uphold the lower courts, a "fallback" budget procedure is specified in the new law. The findings of the CBO and the OMB concerning program cuts under the automatic formula will be given not to the comptroller general and then to the president for automatic execution, but to Congress itself. The findings will be converted into a joint resolution to be considered by Congress on an up or down vote under expedited procedures and, if passed, sent to the president for his signature. Since the sequestration formula specifies that about half the required spending cuts would come from defense, it is probable that the president would veto the joint resolution. Thus it is unlikely that a large deficit reduction will be made through the application of the fallback procedure. Congress and the president, nevertheless, will continue to be under political pressure to achieve the deficit targets they have set for themselves.

There are three major strategies for reaching those targets, and we discuss each of them below.

The Gramm-Rudman-Hollings Alternative

The new budget law can be regarded both as a doomsday machine and as a strategy for deficit reduction embodying four main principles:

— deficits are to be reduced to target levels by reducing spending, not by increasing revenues;

— certain high-priority programs are to be exempt from cuts or given especially favorable treatment;

— the required cut in the remaining programs is to be divided equally between defense and domestic programs;

— within defense and the remaining domestic programs, cuts are to be proportional across the board.

As may be seen in table 3-3, protected programs include social security and certain programs of assistance to the poor, the unemployed, or veterans. Cuts in certain medical programs and student loans are strictly limited, and reductions in pensions for federal employees cannot exceed cost-of-living adjustments. These exemptions and limitations reflect a carefully negotiated agreement in Congress about what areas should or should not be protected partially or completely from spending cuts. In addition, of course, interest on the debt is exempt.

The net result is that less than half the budget—defense plus the unprotected civilian programs—is subject to the full brunt of the spending cuts. This in turn means that cuts in defense and in unprotected domestic programs have to be proportionately higher than would be necessary if the cuts could be spread over a substantially larger fraction of federal spending.

Each year, initially in August and finally in October, the CBO and the OMB are required under the new law to estimate jointly, on the basis of the most recent budgetary actions of Congress, the deficit expected in the coming fiscal year. If that deficit exceeds the Gramm-Rudman-Hollings target, the sequestration procedure would be triggered.[5] Half of the total required spending reductions would be assigned to the defense budget and half to civilian

5. As noted earlier, if the projected deficit in any year is less than $10 billion higher than the targets, the automatic sequestration procedure is not triggered.

Table 3-3. *Budget Outlays as Categorized in Gramm-Rudman-Hollings, Fiscal Year 1986*[a]
Billions of dollars

Spending category	Outlays
Total outlays	**998**
Defense	**275**
Civilian	**633**
Exempt from cuts[b]	295
Subject to limited cuts[c]	87
Subject to elimination of cost-of-living adjustments[d]	48
Unprotected programs	203
Net interest	**139**
Offsetting receipts	**−49**
Addendum	
Total outlays subject to full cuts (defense plus	
unprotected civilian)	478

Sources: CBO, *Economic and Budget Outlook;* and authors' estimates.
  a. The outlays shown here are estimates of spending before the application of the 1986 Gramm-Rudman-Hollings cuts.
  b. Social security and railroad retirement, food stamps and child nutrition, medicaid, welfare programs (aid to families with dependent children and supplemental security income for the aged and disabled), veterans' compensation and pensions, and unemployment compensation.
  c. Medicare, veterans' and other health care, and student loans.
  d. Principally federal military and civilian pensions.

programs. The baseline from which the cuts are taken would depend on the appropriations Congress had already passed; where new appropriation bills had not been enacted, the prior year's appropriations would form the base. It is, of course, impossible to guess what the baseline would be since the imminence of sequestration would itself influence congressional behavior. For example, to the extent that a group of congressmen believes the automatic formula will ultimately be triggered, they have strong incentives *not* to agree during the normal budget process to a cut in any program they particularly favor, since such action would simply lower the baseline for that program from which a later automatic cut would be taken. But whatever the baseline turned out to be, a single percentage reduction calculated by the CBO and the OMB would be uniformly applied to the new budget authority for every program, project, and activity in the defense budget, and another uniform percentage reduction would be applied to the unprotected civilian programs to achieve the required overall spending reduction for that year.[6]

Applying the automatic formula to the defense budget over the next three years would introduce major distortions into the country's military establishment and substantially weaken the readiness of American armed forces. Suppose, for example, that the 1987 cuts in the budget deficit below the CBO current policy baseline (column C of table 3-1) have to be made by applying the automatic formula. In the case of defense, the CBO's current policy projection already assumes no further real growth in the budget beyond the 1986 level (which, in turn, was itself reduced under the Gramm-Rudman-Hollings procedure). To achieve the 1987 objective, an additional $15 billion would have to be taken out of defense spending; to meet the 1989 target, some $27 billion. The reduction must be applied uniformly to a highly detailed list of spending categories. Except in 1986, the president has no authority to reallocate the cuts among categories. As a consequence it would be necessary by 1989 to decrease spending on military personnel in each of the three armed forces by about 9 percent, and, since the law does not allow pay cuts, the size of the armed forces would have to be reduced by almost one-tenth, or 200,000 people.[7] Similarly, training and supplies that are critical in determining the fighting capability of the armed services and their readiness to fight would have to be cut indiscriminately.

Over the past five years there has been a rapid buildup in the procurement of complex weapons systems—ships, planes, tanks, artillery, antitank weapons, and the like. The stock of equipment continues to grow rapidly. The rise in training and operating costs that make it possible to use effectively the growing stock of equipment lags behind the growth in the spending on equipment itself. One way to slow or halt the growth in the defense budget without harming military effectiveness would be to slow the growth of the equipment stockpile by cutting the money for new procurement sharply, while making much smaller cuts, if any at

6. In the case of defense, the percentage reduction would also be applied to prior years' budget authority that had not yet been used by the Pentagon to place new orders for military procurement—that is, "unobligated budget authority."

7. If pay could be cut, its impact on enlistments and reenlistments would also result in a reduction in the size of the armed forces.

all, in the funds for training, operation, maintenance, and related items. The uniform percentage reduction called for in the new law inevitably means that a large part of the earlier buildup in new weapons will have been pure waste, since the armed services will simply not be able to man and deploy them effectively.

In order to ensure that the president would have no discretion to allocate the cuts to meet his own priorities, Congress specified in excruciating detail, for both defense and civilian programs, individual subcategories of spending, each of which would have to be cut by precisely the same percentage. Not only is every individual budget account a separate item, but within each account further subcategorization is required. In the case of the Agriculture Department, every county extension office and every agricultural research station is a separate item. Merely to list the 1986 civilian cuts by budget account, without providing detail for the subcategories, took 126 pages of the *Federal Register*.

Applying to this mass of individual items the sizable equiproportional reductions that would be required over the next three years under the Gramm-Rudman-Hollings formula would give rise to innumerable unintended results. Important aspects of the country's economic life depend on one form or another of federal activities. Especially noticeable are measures that relate to health and safety: air traffic control, maritime safety, regulation of drugs, meat and poultry inspection, nuclear reactor safety regulations, communicable disease information and control, and so on down the list. While one can reasonably argue about the extent to which a period of austerity might induce greater efficiency in these activities, long periods of substantial underfunding would soon produce a stockpile of disasters waiting to happen.

Specialized law enforcement activities carried out by federal agencies such as the Federal Bureau of Investigation, the Internal Revenue Service, customs and immigration, the federal prison system, and the Secret Service would also be hampered. Less dramatic, but still important, would be the deteriorating quality of national parks, wildlife refuges, and similar elements of the national heritage. Moreover, while social security, veterans' compensation, unemployment insurance, and similar cash benefit programs are protected, funds for the administration of each would be cut along with funds for other government operations. Long delays in dealing with inequities, correcting mistakes, and adjudicating disputes would become commonplace. It is not hard to understand why most members of Congress feel that activation of the automatic formula ought to be avoided under virtually any circumstances.

The consequences of applying the detailed sequestration process in fiscal 1987 and beyond would be so devastating to both the military and civilian activities of the federal government that it is almost impossible to imagine Congress and the president allowing them to occur. But if Congress wished to use its normal budgetary procedure to cut spending by enough to meet the deficit targets, the broad allocation of priorities provided in the new law—as opposed to its detailed sequestration mechanics—offers a reasonable guide as to where the cuts would have to be made. Congress would clearly have to cut both defense and civilian programs substantially. And it is difficult to believe that from either a political or a substantive standpoint many of the exempt or partially exempt programs under Gramm-Rudman-Hollings can be subjected to very large spending cuts. The programs for the poor have already been pared over the last four years, and further large reductions are seen even by many conservatives as unwarranted. The elimination of one year's cost-of-living allowance in social security benefits would yield some $7 billion in annual savings. Some such modest reduction in social security benefits might, as discussed later in this chapter, be both feasible and desirable in an alternative that levied some sacrifice on most elements in society, including taxpayers. But it is difficult to argue that social security benefits can, or should, be cut significantly more than this. Thus while the sequestration procedure is universally unacceptable, the broad priorities of the formula reflect a realistic evaluation of what programs would be protected by political and substantive reality, and are a good indication of how deep and how concentrated the cuts would have to be if all the required deficit reductions were to be achieved by spending reductions.

Table 3-4 sets forth, in dollars of constant purchasing power, the budgetary consequences of congressional actions that would

Table 3-4. *Budget Outlays for Selected Fiscal Years, 1981–89, with Spending Cuts in 1987 and 1989 Allocated According to Gramm-Rudman-Hollings Provisions*[a]

Billions of 1986 dollars unless otherwise specified

Spending category	1981	1986 (before cuts)	1987	1989	Percent change		
					1981–86	1986–89	1981–89
Total outlays[a]	**844**	**998**	**950**	**943**	**18**	**–6**	**12**
Defense	197	275	259	252	40	–8	28
Interest	86	139	138	132	62	–5	53
Civilian							
Protected under GRH	387	430	432	449	11	4	16
Unprotected under GRH	224	203	171	161	–9	–21	–28
Offsetting receipts	–49	–49	–50	–51	…	…	…

Source: CBO, *Economic and Budget Outlook.* CBO projections of current service outlays adjusted by author to reflect spending reductions allocated along the broad lines set forth in the Gramm-Rudman-Hollings (GRH) law. Details in this and subsequent tables may not add to totals because of rounding.

a. In allocating the cuts it was assumed that the general revenue sharing law would be allowed to expire and the remaining cuts divided equally between defense and civilian programs.

meet the deficit targets solely through spending cuts allocated along the broad lines laid down in Gramm-Rudman-Hollings.[8]

The results depend, of course, on the baseline from which the cuts are made. Suppose that baseline were the February CBO budget projection. In the case of the defense budget, a little less than half of the $37 billion and $72 billion of cuts needed in fiscal 1987 and 1989 respectively would be taken out of a defense budget that had already been reduced by the 1986 cuts and had not risen thereafter. The real growth in defense spending that has so far characterized the 1980s would be halted and partially reversed. By 1989 about 29 percent of the buildup from 1981 to 1986 would be eliminated (that is, the $78 billion rise would be pared back by $23 billion). The defense budget in 1989 would end up at about the same level as would have been reached from a continuation throughout the 1980s of the 3 percent a year growth planned by the Carter administration.

The unprotected civilian programs have already been cut 9 percent in absolute terms during the past five years. Between 1986 and 1989, under the alternative we are now discussing, spending on these programs would fall another 21 percent to about a third below what it was at the beginning of the decade. But the cuts would not be proportional. Within the overall total of unprotected programs, some are more unprotected than others. A 15 to 20 percent slash in the Internal Revenue Service budget would arouse taxpayers' ire over delayed refunds and might indeed lead to substantially reduced tax collection. Congress will not sharply cut air traffic control, or the maritime safety activities of the Coast Guard, or the reactor safety program of the Nuclear Regulatory Commission. Once allowances are made for a large number of such situations, very substantial cuts would be necessary for many of the remaining civilian activities of the federal government.

If the allocation of cuts were made not from the CBO baseline, but from a baseline that allowed for 3 percent real growth in defense budget authority, the 1989 budget allocation would be as follows:

---

8. The inflation adjustment (the change in the price deflator for the gross national product) is the same for each category of spending. This does not imply that prices actually rise by exactly the same amount in each category. But adjusting each one by the same GNP deflator provides a measure of how much generalized purchasing power has to be given up by the nation to support the particular category or program.

	Billions of constant dollars	Percentage change 1986–89
Defense	260	− 5
Civilian		
Protected	449	4
Unprotected	154	− 23

The decline in defense spending from current levels would then be very small, but the difference would have to be made up by a massive further slash in all of the unprotected programs, taking them down by 23 percent (on top of the 9 percent cut between 1981 and 1986).

The Administration's Proposal

In his budget plan delivered to Congress early this year, the president set forth his proposals to meet the Gramm-Rudman-Hollings deficit target over the next five years.[9] He intends to sell government-owned financial and other assets at a rate of some $3.5 billion a year and to request several small tax increases averaging about $5 billion a year. (The special issues raised by the administration's program of asset sales are discussed in the appendix to this chapter.) But to accomplish the bulk of the reduction, he proposes to

— restore most of the $14 billion cut from defense budget authority in 1986 and increase defense budget authority by 3 percent a year in inflation-adjusted terms;

— leave social security benefits untouched, but make substan-

9. This section of the chapter uses the CBO's estimates both for baseline spending and for the spending effects of the administration's deficit-reducing proposals. See *An Analysis of the President's Budgetary Proposals for Fiscal Year 1987* (CBO, 1986). The CBO assumes that the proceeds of the administration's proposed sale of the governmentally owned power administrations will be realized on a very different time schedule than that assumed by the administration, particularly in 1989. (The CBO estimates that most of the proceeds will be realized at time of sale; the administration spreads the receipts out over time.) As a consequence the annual estimates of assets sales in this chapter and its appendix are quite different from those included in the administration's budget. The CBO estimate of the sum of the proceeds over a number of years, however, is not very much different from that of the administration. Finally, in 1988 and later years the CBO estimates of the defense spending that would result from the administration's budget proposals are slightly lower than the CBO estimates of the consequences of restoring the 1986 cuts and providing 3 percent real growth in budget authority.

tial reductions amounting to $11 billion in 1987 and $23 billion in 1989 in other protected programs;

— cut $14 billion in 1987 and $28 billion in 1989 in the unprotected programs (an additional $3 billion to $4 billion a year would be recovered in increases in fees charged the public for the use of various federal government services);

— make selective spending cuts, including the outright abolition of a number of programs, rather than apply equiproportional reductions to all programs and activities.

According to the Congressional Budget Office and outside budget experts, the spending that would be forthcoming from the proposed defense budget authority is understated by some $14 billion in fiscal 1987 and a total of $64 billion over the five fiscal years 1987–91.[10] In addition, estimates of interest payments on the public debt in the president's budget are predicated on an assumed steady reduction in short-term interest rates to 4.8 percent in 1989 and 4 percent in 1991. This reduction, in turn, appears to be closely associated with an assumed decline in inflation to 3.2 percent in 1989 and 2.0 percent in 1991. A more realistic estimate of inflation and interest rates would produce a higher level of federal expenditures. The CBO projection of short-term interest rates, 6.1 percent by 1989 and 5.4 percent by 1991, seems a more prudent basis on which to make budget policy. On both counts—understated defense spending and excessively optimistic interest rates—the reductions in civilian spending required to meet the deficit targets, given the administration's proposed rise in the defense budget, would have to be much larger than those called for by the president's 1987 budget. In addition, as spelled out in the appendix, selling off the federal government's assets as a way of reducing the budget deficit does not accomplish the economic purposes of deficit reduction. Hence, to meet the deficit targets in an economically meaningful way while continuing to pursue its basic budget strategy, the administration would have to find still further outlay cuts in civilian programs. Those additional spending cuts would have to amount to $18 billion and $28 billion in fiscal years 1987 and 1989 respectively.

Using the baseline projection of the deficit as it would be

10. CBO, *An Analysis of the President's Budgetary Proposals*, pp. 27–32. See also Joshua M. Epstein, *The 1987 Defense Budget* (Brookings, forthcoming).

Table 3-5. *Administration's Proposals to Reduce the Budget Deficit, Fiscal Years 1987 and 1989*
Billions of dollars

Item	1987	1989
Baseline deficit (before GRH 1986 cuts; 3 percent defense growth)[a]	**202**	**187**
Spending changes	−31	−62
Part of 1986 GRH cuts[b]	−7	−12
Additional civilian spending cuts	−24	−50
GRH protected programs	−10	−22
Other programs	−14	−28
User fees[c]	−3	−6
Tax increases	−6	−9
Asset sales[d]	−2	−9
Interest savings	−1	−11
Resulting deficit	**160**	**91**
GRH deficit target	**144**	**72**
Addendum		
Additional reductions required to offset underestimates in defense spending and to substitute for asset sales	18	28

Sources: CBO, *An Analysis of the President's Budgetary Proposals for Fiscal Year 1987* (GPO, 1986); *The Budget of the United States Government, Fiscal Year 1987.*
a. From column A, table 3-1.
b. The president's budget retains all of the 1986 Gramm-Rudman-Hollings cuts for civilian programs but only a small fraction of those for defense programs. See note 9.
c. Includes proposed increase in medicare beneficiary premium.
d. The administration assumes that the proceeds from the sale of the Bonneville Power Administration are spread out over a number of years, while the CBO assumes that those proceeds are all realized in fiscal 1989.

without the 1986 cuts and with 3 percent real growth in the defense budget, table 3-5 shows how the administration proposes to meet the deficit targets, and estimates the further spending cuts that would be required if defense outlays and interest payments have indeed been understated by the administration.

The levels of spending implied in the administration's proposals, arranged according to the Gramm-Rudman-Hollings categories and expressed in dollars of today's purchasing power are shown in the top part of table 3-6. The table also shows the additional cuts in civilian programs that would be necessary to meet the deficit targets once the administration's understatement of defense spending and interest payments is corrected. Purely for illustrative purposes these additional cuts are allocated among protected and unprotected programs in the same ratio as the cuts already proposed by the administration.

In the administration's budget, real defense spending would continue to grow at a rate of 3 percent a year plus an amount to make up for most of the 1986 cuts.[11] The growth in spending for protected civilian programs would slow sharply; to meet the deficit targets fully, it would have to cease altogether.

The major programs that are protected under Gramm-Rudman-Hollings but are cut rather sharply by the administration are medicare, medicaid, and student loans. Under the new law, cuts in medicare, the program of health care for the elderly, are limited to increases of only 2 percent a year on reimbursements for physicians and hospitals, saving $4 billion a year by 1989. The administration proposes a variety of devices to lower payments to health care suppliers and save $6.7 billion a year by 1989. In addition, the administration hopes to get Congress to agree to raise the monthly premium that beneficiaries pay for medicare physicians' services. When medicare first began, these premiums covered 50 percent of costs while the federal government covered the rest. The premium was supposed to keep up with rising costs so that the 50 percent ratio would be maintained. But over the years Congress has limited the rise in premiums so that they now cover only 25 percent of costs. The administration proposes to raise the premiums gradually until they cover 35 percent of costs. Together with other increases in beneficiary payments for health care services, an additional $3.9 billion a year would be collected by 1989. Proposals to raise the premium are not new. In recent years, administrations of both political parties have regularly made them to Congress—to no avail.

The administration cuts in medicaid, the program of medical assistance for the poor, would come principally from putting a cap on allowable payments to the states, who run the medicaid program with federal financial aid. Federal spending for the program would fall by $1.2 billion in 1987 and $3.3 billion in 1989.

11. The CBO has estimated the annual defense spending that would occur in 1987–91 if the administration's request and future plans for budget authority in those years were granted. Starting in 1988 these spending estimates run slightly below the CBO estimate of what the consequences would be if the 1986 spending cuts were restored and real defense budget authority grew by 3 percent a year.

Table 3-6. Budget Outlays for Selected Fiscal Years, 1981–89, with Spending Cuts in 1987 and 1989 Allocated According to the Administration's Proposal
Billions of 1986 dollars unless otherwise specified

Spending category	1981	1986 (before cuts)	1987	1989	Percent change 1981–86	Percent change 1986–89	Percent change 1981–89
With cuts proposed in 1987 budget message							
Total outlays	**844**	**998**	**970**	**968**	**18**	**-3**	**15**
Defense	197	275	286	298	40	8	51
Interest	86	139	138	136	62	-2	58
Civilian							
Protected under GRH	387	430	424	438	11	2	13
Unprotected under GRH	224	203	176	161	-9	-21	-28
Offsetting receipts[a]	-49	-49	-54	-66	...	...	...
With cuts sufficient to meet GRH targets[b]							
Civilian							
Protected under GRH	387	430	416	429	10	0	10
Unprotected under GRH	224	203	166	149	-9	-27	-33

Sources: See table 3-5.

a. If spending were decreased to replace the proceeds for the administration's proposed asset sales program, as shown in the bottom half of the table, "offsetting receipts" would be $52 billion in 1987 and $57 billion in 1989. Total spending in 1989 would be $961 billion in fiscal 1986 dollars.

b. Because the administration has underestimated spending on defense and interest, meeting the Gramm-Rudman-Hollings targets (without relying on sales of assets) would require spending cuts greater than those proposed in the president's budget. The additional cuts are assumed to be distributed between protected and unprotected programs in the same proportion as they are in the original administration proposal.

Cuts in the federal student loan program would rise to $2.6 billion in 1989—a 30 percent reduction. The savings would come principally from tightening eligibility requirements for subsidized loans and requiring parents to pay a higher fraction of schooling costs before subsidies are made available.

Less so than under Gramm-Rudman-Hollings, but still in a very substantial way, the largest proportional cutback under the administration's budget is in spending for the unprotected category of programs. Because the administration has apparently underestimated the spending consequences of its budgetary program and because it wants to make some of the civilian budget cuts in the protected programs, the amount it proposes to cut out of the unprotected programs is about the same as would occur if the Gramm-Rudman-Hollings allocation of cuts were imposed (compare tables 3-4 and 3-6). But if the administration's spending cuts were sufficiently large to achieve the targets in an economically meaningful way—that is, if the spending underestimates noted earlier were corrected and the asset sales program eliminated— the unprotected programs would have to be cut more, by some 33 percent from 1981 to 1989, rather than the 28 percent required by Gramm-Rudman-Hollings. Meeting the deficit targets solely through civilian spending cuts would bring the 1989 inflation-adjusted level of spending on unprotected civilian programs to a point 35 percent below what it was at the beginning of the decade.

Unlike the across-the-board approach to spending cuts contemplated in the Gramm-Rudman-Hollings formula, the administration's cuts are—wisely, we think—selective. While the Gramm-Rudman-Hollings law explicitly precludes the termination of any program, the administration proposes either to end or to curtail drastically a number of government activities. The credit programs of the Small Business Administration and the Economic Development Administration would be eliminated and a number of other smaller programs terminated for a saving of about $2 billion in 1987 and $3.5 billion in 1989. Merchant marine subsidies would be cut and subsidies to Amtrak, the country's passenger rail service, would be ended. Amtrak's passenger revenues now cover such a small fraction of operating costs (45 percent) that ending the subsidy would throw the service into bankruptcy. Conceivably, passenger service along the northeast corridor and a few other densely populated short routes could be continued profitably under private ownership. Other services would undoubtedly disappear for lack of sufficient passenger demand.

In addition to its cuts in the protected medicare, medicaid, and student loan programs, the administration proposes large reductions in a wide range of other social programs, amounting to $3.5 billion in 1987 and $5.5 billion in 1989. Job training and income assistance programs, which principally serve the poor, would be cut sharply, with the cuts growing to $2.5 billion by 1989. In the health field, the administration would limit admission to veterans' hospitals to servicemen with service-connected disabilities, cut biomedical research by $400 million in 1987 and $800 million in 1989, and cut training subsidies for the health professions. Although labeled as part of its "privatization" efforts, a large reduction in housing subsidies for low- and moderate-income families is also proposed, combined with a major, and possibly desirable, change in the form of the subsidy. Instead of contracting through local governments or nonprofit organizations for the construction of new subsidized housing units, the administration proposes to offer to potential low- and moderate-income residents housing vouchers, payments designed to enable them to rent private housing of a quality they could not otherwise afford, for a saving of some $4 billion in 1987 and $6 billion in 1989.

The administration also proposes reductions of $1 billion in 1987 and $5 billion in 1989 in other grant-in-aid programs operated by state and local governments. In addition, the administration is not asking for extension of the $4.4-billion-a-year program of general revenue sharing, which expires in 1987. Federal grants to state and local governments (apart from those used for medicaid and income security), measured in billions of dollars of 1986 purchasing power, have already been cut severely and would fall even further under the administration's proposals, as shown below.

Grants to States and Localities
(excluding medicaid and income security)

1981	1987	1989	Percent change 1981–89
73	48	41	−44

In a number of cases the programs that the administration proposes to reduce or eliminate generate benefits to the nation that are smaller than their costs. While the political opposition to such cuts from well-organized beneficiaries and their representatives is fierce, the cuts make good sense on substantive grounds. It is hard to justify deep taxpayer subsidies for sparsely patronized long distance passenger trains or for continued large subsidies to merchant shipping. For many years presidents have tried to curtail taxpayer provision of hospital beds for veterans with illnesses in no way connected to their military service. Subsidized and guaranteed loans for rural electrification are a holdover from the 1930s. Now, with 99 percent of American farms electrified, the Rural Electrification Administration continues to lend hundreds of millions a year, sometimes at interest rates of 5 percent.

In the case of grants-in-aid to state and local governments, many of the administration's proposals consist of two elements. First, various reforms in the nature of the grants are being put forward, generally in the desirable direction of increasing the flexibility allowed states and localities in their use of the money. In the case of transportation, the federal government now heavily subsidizes the capital cost of mass transit systems, giving local authorities every incentive to build excessively grandiose and capital-intensive systems. Reform of the grants to allow much more diversified use of the funds would reduce the incentives for inefficiency. But the administration is proposing to couple sensible reforms in the nature of the grants with severe cuts in their size. Given the large reductions that have already been made in federal grants to state and local governments and the imminent demise of general revenue sharing, cuts of this severity coming in the next several years will place major strains on the finances of state and local governments. Provision of many services will not simply be shifted to state and local taxpayers. The services will not be provided at all. Moreover, the magnitude of the cuts is likely to jeopardize the president's chances of getting the legislation necessary to introduce the desirable reforms.

Some of the changes proposed for medicaid, housing subsidies, and other social services may indeed be warranted. But taken altogether, the reductions that are proposed in these programs cut further into a base of support for the poor that has already been eroded significantly.

In sum, the administration has put forth a number of sensible cuts and reforms in the subsidies that the government now provides to selected industries, services, and interests.[12] Politically, if history is a guide, Congress is unlikely to accept most of them, preferring to cut many programs evenhandedly rather than performing selective and radical budgetary surgery where it would do the most good. With respect both to social service programs and to grants-in-aid to states and localities, the administration has proposed some well-designed reforms, but placed them in the context of large funding reductions that come on top of earlier ones. The wisdom and political viability of those cuts are highly questionable.

Finally, Congress is not only unlikely to accept the magnitude or distribution of the president's proposed civilian spending cuts, it is even more unlikely to accept the further cuts that will be required to compensate for the administration's unrealistically low estimates of defense spending and interest payments.

A Third Alternative

Several facts stand out from this examination of the budget problem.

First, with respect to the defense budget, agreement not to restore the cuts in budget authority made in 1986 would lower defense spending some $11 billion in 1989. If Congress decided to allow no further growth in real budget authority for defense, spending would fall an additional $3 billion in 1987 and $18 billion in 1989 below the path of 3 percent real growth contained in last year's budget resolution. The defense budget totals would then be as follows, in billions of dollars:

	1987	1989
Defense outlays with 3 percent real growth after 1986	296	340
Effect of 1986 cuts	−9	−11
Effect of zero real growth	−3	−18
Resulting defense outlays	284	311

12. See table 3-8 for a partial list of programs chosen from the administration's proposals and recommended as prime candidates for reduction or elimination.

According to a forthcoming study by Joshua M. Epstein, a reasonable defense posture could be maintained with spending at a level somewhat below those totals, or about $300 billion by 1989.[13] Epstein examines the objectives and missions of the armed forces for strategic deterrence and conventional war and concludes that they could be met effectively with a smaller military budget. Given the very large buildup in defense procurement that has occurred over the past five years, he argues that procurement of a number of weapons ought to be stretched out over a longer time and that some weapons systems should be cancelled. Growth should be preserved, however, in most of the operation and maintenance programs. After the stretch-outs and cancellations the stock of military weapons will still grow and require additional funds for effective deployment by the armed forces. Those funds could be provided in the zero-growth budget.

Even conservatively evaluated, it would thus be possible to set the defense budget on a path of zero real growth, as shown above, while maintaining a strong and improving defense capability. Some modest additional cuts might also be feasible. But large additional cuts along the lines that would be required under the Gramm-Rudman-Hollings allocation formula would run the risk of lowering the country's military capabilities. In particular, large reductions from the CBO baseline budget in funds for operation and maintenance could well render useless some of the buildup in military weaponry that has already occurred.

Second, it appeared last fall that it would take $115 billion in spending cuts or tax increases to achieve the 1989 target of a deficit no higher than $72 billion (see table 3–2). Now, starting from the latest CBO baseline, it would take only $72 billion of budgetary actions to meet the 1989 goal. Defense and civilian budget cuts amounting to some $43 billion have either been put into effect already or would be made if Congress appropriated defense funds on the basis of the CBO baseline of zero real growth, as outlined above.

Third, as suggested by our review of the administration's budget reduction proposals, some further civilian budget cuts may be warranted, but meeting the targets solely by civilian spending cuts

13. Epstein, *The 1987 Defense Budget.*

is neither substantively desirable nor politically feasible. Cutting the budget along the broad allocations set forth in Gramm-Rudman-Hollings—half defense and half civilian—would be too severe on both defense and civilian budgets if the cuts were taken from the new CBO baseline for defense. And if taken from a higher defense baseline, the required cuts in civilian programs would then be extremely large and even further beyond what is substantively or politically feasible.

Fourth, some civilian programs of the federal government, especially those in the unprotected category, have already been cut significantly in recent years. Outside of defense, social security, and interest payments on the debt, the share of the GNP flowing to the other programs of the federal government has fallen substantially since 1981 (see table 3-7). A good bit of that decline was healthy; it eliminated some of the excesses built up in the 1960s and 1970s. But there were also some unwanted casualties. In the furious search to hold down the budget deficit, a wide range of day-to-day federal activities that play a major role in the economic and social life of the nation have been starved for operating funds.

The buying power of federal funds for support of nondefense research and development has been significantly eroded, to the long-run detriment of the nation's potential for technological advance. Federal support for job training programs has fallen substantially. And in the six years between fiscal years 1981 and 1987 the real purchasing power of grants to states for social services—principally for the poor—will have fallen more than 20 percent. The medicaid program, while far from perfectly designed and run, has virtually wrought a revolution in making health care available to the poor, who previously had lagged far behind the rest of the population in their access to health care. Yet between 1977 and 1984, the number of children receiving medicaid assistance dropped by over 20 percent relative to the number of children living in poverty.

Recently there has been a renewal of a much earlier public debate about whether federal welfare payments help the people they are supposed to help or create incentives and attitudes that, in the long run, perpetuate poverty, especially among female-headed families in inner cities. Largely unnoticed in this debate

Table 3-7. *Trends in Selected Components of Federal Revenues and Outlays, Fiscal Years 1960–89*
Percent of GNP

					1989	
Component	1960–69	1970–79	1981	1986[a]	Baseline[b]	Recommended[c]
Revenues	18.2	18.3	20.1	18.6	19.0	20.0
General	15.5	14.0	14.6	12.6	12.7	13.7
Social security[d]	2.7	4.3	5.5	6.0	6.3	6.3
Outlays	19.0	20.4	22.7	23.5	22.6	21.3
Defense	8.9	6.0	5.3	6.4	6.6	6.0
Net interest	1.3	1.5	2.3	3.3	3.1	2.9
Social security[e]	2.8	4.7	6.1	6.5	6.6	6.4
Other	6.0	8.2	9.0	7.3	6.2	6.1

Sources: Historical Tables, The Budget of the United States Government, Fiscal Year 1987; CBO, Economic and Budget Outlook.
a. Before 1986 Gramm-Rudman-Hollings cuts.
b. Baseline budget, before Gramm-Rudman-Hollings, 3 percent real defense growth. Consistent with deficit shown in column A of table 3-1.
c. Budget after carrying out recommended program of tax increases and spending cuts. See table 3-13.
d. Includes hospital insurance tax.
e. Includes medicare outlays.

are the facts that the real purchasing power of cash benefits per family in aid to families with dependent children (AFDC), the largest federal welfare program, fell 15 percent between 1974 and 1984 and that the percentage of children in poverty whose families receive AFDC payments dropped from 79 in 1974 to 55 in 1984. Whatever the outcome of the debate about cash welfare payments and the wisdom of lowering benefits and tightening eligibility, reducing the provision of job training and health care services to the nation's poor is not likely to be the route by which progress is made in solving the problems.

In combination, the reductions in the value of cash benefits, job training, and health and social services have substantially lowered federal assistance to the poor. Some of the recent cuts were warranted and some abuses corrected. But in the process, and in the general pressure of the budget squeeze, some cuts were too large, and some improvements that might have been made at moderate cost were foregone. Even viewed conservatively there are some areas of national life outside of military security in which the federal government has an important role to play. Operating year in and year out under the rule that less is always better does not produce an efficient or appropriate use of national resources. Efficient budgeting does indeed require a tough and skeptical attitude toward requests to spend the taxpayers' money. But it also requires that modest funds be available to finance new or expanded activities that, after tough-minded review, promise to generate national gains larger than their costs.

All of these considerations suggest an approach to meeting the deficit targets along the following lines.

First, of the $115 billion in budgetary actions needed to reduce last year's deficit projections to the deficit targets by 1989, almost 20 percent has already been achieved through spending reductions. Another 20 percent would be realized by keeping the real level of defense budget authority constant over the next three or four years. A substantial share of the remaining deficit reductions should come through tax increases.

Second, in the list of reductions proposed by the administration, cuts of at least $6 billion to $8 billion in 1987, growing to $15 billion or more by 1989, make good sense in terms of eliminating wasteful programs or reducing uneconomic and socially unjustifiable subsidies. An illustrative list of administration-proposed cuts is shown in table 3-8. From this list of candidates, cuts of $15 billion can and should be found.

Third, under a plan in which taxpayers are being asked to accept a tax increase and spending programs already diminished by cuts are being cut further, it would be fair and quite probably politically feasible to ask social security recipients to take a small reduction in the net value of their benefits. The fairest way to enact the change would be to subject half of social security benefits to the income tax.[14] Social security recipients with incomes over $32,000 already pay such a tax.[15] Removing the income limitation could raise an additional $7 billion a year. Alternatively, but less desirably, eliminating for two years one-half of the cost-of-living

14. Since half of the payroll taxes that support social security are paid by workers from their before-tax income, taxing more than half of their retirement or other social security benefits could be considered double taxation.

15. $25,000 for single people.

Table 3-8. *Potential Cuts in Low-Priority Federal Civilian Programs, Fiscal Year 1989*
Billions of dollars

Program	Cut
Medicare (half of administration proposal)	5.0
User fees[a]	4.3
Civil service retirement (half of administration proposal)	1.5
Small Business Administration and Economic Development Administration	2.0
Veterans' medical care	1.4
Subsidy to Amtrak	0.7
Other subsidies (maritime subsidies, various credit programs)	0.8
General revenue sharing	4.6

Source: *Budget of the United States Government, Fiscal Year 1987.*
a. Of these cuts, $1 billion would show up as increased revenues and the rest as "offsetting receipts," which reduce budget expenditures.

adjustment under social security would produce budget savings of about the same amount by 1989.[16]

Fourth, while spending for a number of civilian programs should be cut, some programs that serve important needs of the nation have been cut too far, as briefly spelled out above. A modest sum—$4 billion in 1987, rising to perhaps $8 billion to $10 billion in 1989—ought to be applied on a highly selective basis toward restoring and improving those programs. An illustrative list of high-priority uses for such funds is given in table 3-9. Funds for program expansion should be made available, however, only by reallocation from cuts made in other areas of the budget as recommended above. They should on no account be made at the expense of keeping the deficit above the Gramm-Rudman-Hollings targets.

Finally, a tax increase that yielded $50 billion in 1989, together with the cuts and reallocations in federal spending and in social security benefits outlined above, would meet the deficit targets, as shown in table 3-10. The tax increase would raise by almost 1 percentage point the share in GNP of federal general revenues

16. Military and civilian federal government retirees lost one full year of cost-of-living allowance in the 1986 Gramm-Rudman-Hollings cuts.

Table 3-9. *Proposals to Increase Spending on Federal Civilian Programs, Fiscal Year 1989*
Billions of dollars

Proposal	Spending increase
Restore 1981 purchasing power of Head Start, Job Corps, summer youth employment, education for the handi- capped, the work-incentive program, and social service grants to states	1.9
Restore 1981 purchasing power of civilian research and development[a]	2.8
Expand medicaid eligibility among the working poor and improve minimum medicaid and cash benefit standards	2.0
Increase block grants to states for job training programs to provide work, skills, and job opportunities for welfare recipients[b]	1.8
Increase funding for federal aviation and maritime safety activities, operation of the national parks, Federal Bureau of Prisons, and federal border control activities	0.7

Source: Authors' estimates.
a. Excluding the National Aeronautics and Space Administration.
b. Funds provided would restore programs to two-thirds of their 1981 real purchasing levels.

(that is, all federal revenues except the payroll taxes dedicated to social security and medicare).

If this program were adopted, it would change the shape of the budget as shown in the last column of table 3-7. In 1989, budget outlays would fall to 21.3 percent of GNP—more than 2 percentage points lower than in 1986 and approximately the same share of GNP as in the last half of the 1970s. The substantial rise in social security benefits and interest payments as a share of GNP occurring between the end of the 1970s and the end of the 1980s would be completely financed by a reduction in the share of GNP taken by other civilian spending. Under the recommended alternative, the share of "other civilian" spending in GNP would, by 1989, fall to its 1960s level. On the tax side the recommended program would, as noted, raise general revenues by 1 percentage point above their current share of GNP, but leave that share at a lower level than in 1981 or any other time since the beginning of World War II.

Table 3-10. *Recommended Alternative to Reduce the Budget Deficit, Fiscal Years 1987 and 1989*
Billions of dollars

Item	1987	1989
Baseline deficit (before GRH 1986 cuts;		
3 percent defense growth)[a]	**202**	**187**
Spending changes	−26	−50
1986 GRH cuts (defense and civilian)	−16	−19
Zero real defense growth	−3	−18
Additional cuts in civilian programs	−9	−15
Increases in civilian programs	4	9
Net reduction in social security benefits[b]	−2	−7
Tax increases	−30	−50
Interest savings	−2	−15
Resulting deficit	**144**	**72**
Addendum		
Total defense spending cuts	−12	−29
Total civilian cuts (net of increases)	−14	−21

Sources: CBO, *Economic and Budget Outlook;* and authors' estimates.
a. From column A, table 3-1.
b. If the net reduction in social security benefits were accomplished by taxing half of social security benefits (without an income floor), then these amounts would appear as tax increases rather than spending cuts.

Comparison of Alternatives

Table 3-11 shows how spending under the recommended programs, measured in constant dollars, would compare with that in earlier years, and table 3-12 compares the results with those forthcoming under the two alternatives discussed earlier. The recommended alternative keeps defense spending above the level that would result from imposition of the Gramm-Rudman-Hollings cuts, but substantially below that of the administration's defense budget. On the other hand the recommended alternative would cut the programs that are protected under Gramm-Rudman-Hollings although not as much as the administration strategy would.[17] There is a large difference between the recommended

17. The cuts actually proposed by the administration are not as large as implied by the table, but, as noted in the text, to meet the deficit targets the administration would have to find civilian cuts of some $28 billion beyond those it has already proposed in order to offset its large underestimates of budget spending by 1989. We have allocated those additional cuts to protected and unprotected programs in the same ratio as the administration-proposed cuts are allocated.

Table 3-11. *Budget Outlays for Selected Fiscal Years, 1981–89,*
with Spending Cuts in 1987 and 1989 Allocated According
to the Recommended Alternative
Billions of 1986 dollars unless otherwise specified

Spending category	1981	1986 (before cuts)	1987	1989	Percent change 1981–86	1986–89	1981–89
Total outlays	**845**	**998**	**978**	**988**	**18**	**−1**	**17**
Defense	197	275	273	276	40	0	40
Interest	86	139	138	132	62	−1	53
Civilian							
Protected	387	430	430	448	10	4	15
Unprotected	224	203	187	183	−9	−10	−18
Offsetting receipts	−49	−49	−50	−51	...	...	...

Source: Authors' estimates.

alternative and the other two in spending for the unprotected category of programs. Between 1986 and 1989, the recommended alternative would cut those programs by 10 percent, compared with 20 to 30 percent under either of the other two strategies. Politically it seems unlikely that Congress—or the public, once it felt their impact—would permit such cuts to occur. And although a number of major cuts are indeed warranted on substantive grounds, 20 to 30 percent reductions would eliminate too many important social benefits to be acceptable. For both of these reasons, we believe a sizable tax increase is a necessary part in any plan to bring the deficit within range of the target.

Table 3-13 summarizes the budgetary consequences of the three alternatives by showing the share of 1989 GNP taken by revenues and by various categories of outlays under each alternative. Under all three, total government spending as a share of GNP will fall substantially. The recommended alternative keeps revenues at the 1981 share of GNP. It provides for a 2.7 percentage point cut in civilian spending, enough both to accommodate a rise in the share going to defense and interest and to cut the deficit from 2.6 percent of GNP in 1981 to 1.3 percent in 1989. The other proposals would lower revenues another 1 percent of GNP and cut more deeply into spending to make up the difference.

Table 3-12. *Comparison of Budget Outcomes under Three Alternative Ways of Reaching Gramm-Rudman-Hollings Targets, Selected Fiscal Years, 1981–89*
Billions of 1986 dollars

Spending category	1981	1986	GRH[a] A	GRH[a] B	Administration proposal[b]	Recommended alternative
					1989	
Total outlays	**845**	**998**	**943**	**943**	**968**	**988**
Defense	197	275	252	260	298	276
Civilian						
Protected	387	430	449	449	429	448
Unprotected	224	203	161	154	149	183

Source: Authors' estimates.
a. The A version assumes that the cut is imposed from a baseline that incorporates a halt to the real growth in defense budget authority. The B version assumes the cut is made from a baseline that incorporates a 3 percent annual real growth in the defense budget.
b. The administration proposed cuts were augmented to offset the administration's underestimate of defense spending and interest payments on the debt, as explained in the text.

Several other outcomes are quite possible. For example, the impasse may continue; the parties fail to agree on a solution but, for differing reasons, are not willing to accept the consequences of the sequestration formula. Late this year they reach a negotiated settlement that includes some cuts in defense and civilian programs, perhaps several measures to raise modest additional tax revenues, and a postponement of part of the targeted 1987 reduction in the deficit. The deficit falls, but by less than contemplated in Gramm-Rudman-Hollings. The outcome leaves the nation with a deficit that is too high. Financial markets in the United States and around the world now appear to be acting on the assumption that the deficit targets will in large part be met. Some of the recent decline in interest rates stemmed from that belief. Failure of Congress and the president to agree on a means of at least approximating the targets could bring with it a bad reaction in the financial markets and a possible run-up in interest rates, with damaging consequences for the economy that the Federal Reserve might find difficult to handle. For both short-run as well as long-

Table 3-13. *Trends in Selected Components of Federal Revenues
and Outlays, Fiscal Year 1981, and under Three Alternative Budget
Programs, Fiscal Year 1989*
Percent of GNP

		1989		
Component	1981	GRH[a]	Administration proposal[b]	Recommended alternative
Revenues	20.1	19.0	19.2	20.0
General	14.6	12.7	12.9	13.7
Social security	5.5	6.3	6.3	6.3
Outlays[c]	22.7	20.4	20.6	21.3
Defense	5.3	5.4	6.4	6.0
Civilian	16.4	13.2	12.5	13.7
Protected	10.4	9.7	9.2	9.7
Unprotected	6.0	3.5	3.2	4.0
Net interest	2.3	2.9	2.9	2.9
Deficit	−2.6	−1.4	−1.4	−1.3

Sources: Table 3-7; and authors' estimates.
a. Estimate assumes that cuts are made from a baseline that incorporates zero real growth in defense budget authority.
b. Estimate assumes that civilian programs are cut by an amount sufficient to offset the asset sales and the administration's underestimates of defense spending.
c. Total includes "offsetting receipts" not shown separately. The reduction in net social security benefits in the recommended alternative is reflected in lower outlays; if it were done by taxing social security benefits it would show up as a revenue increase. The amount involved is 0.1 percent of GNP.

run economic reasons, that alternative ought to be strongly opposed.

One final alternative is a strategy that patches together some modest spending cuts, small tax increases, and asset sales that will get the 1987 budget deficit within $10 billion of the target, a range that will keep it safe from the Gramm-Rudman-Hollings automatic cuts. If the 1987 deficit can be brought within $10 billion of the target of $144 billion, sequestration will not go into effect. If budget authority for both defense and civilian programs is frozen at 1986 levels and the legislation authorizing general revenue sharing is allowed to expire, the 1987 deficit would be $167 billion, according to the CBO. Only $14 billion more in deficit reduction would be needed. The president has proposed some extensions and small increases in excise taxes and fees and a program for strengthening the IRS to bring in higher tax collections. He has also proposed to sell $2 billion of government-owned assets in 1987. Acceptance of these proposals would reduce the 1987 deficit by $7 billion. Small additional increases in excise taxes and some very modest cuts in spending could bring the fiscal 1987 deficit below $154 billion, the level that would trigger the automatic cuts. There are several serious problems with this strategy, however. The package would still miss the deficit target by $10 billion and would signal that the government was not in fact taking strong action against the deficit. Its $2 billion in asset sales would have no economic impact. And in 1988 and beyond, the deficit problem would remain a very substantial one. Congress and the administration would have succeeded in postponing the solution for one more year. But as the financial markets saw through the strategy and recognized that the deficit had actually been improved much less than anticipated, some reaction by way of higher interest rates could be expected.

Appendix: Selling Public Assets

Two questions should be asked about administration plans to sell public assets. First, in terms of their impact on the economy, should the proceeds from these asset sales count as a part of the deficit reduction? And second, what impact would the sales have on the future operations of government and the size of its future budgets?

The answer to the first question is that the sale of public assets, while reducing the accounting measure of the deficit, does not achieve the economic goals of deficit reduction. Proceeds of the sales of either real or financial assets will have virtually no effect on the government's absorption of funds from financial markets and will do nothing to relieve the upward pressure that high-volume government borrowing exerts on interest rates, private investment, and the trade deficit.

The administration proposes to sell two broad types of assets: financial assets such as mortgages and real assets such as the electricity generating and transmission facilities of the Bonneville Power Administration. From its portfolio of loans and mortgages acquired over the course of many years, the administration plans to sell some $4.4 billion worth to the public in 1987 and even more over the five-year period 1987–91. But for two reasons the net realization to the federal government from these sales will be less than $1 billion over the next five years. First, the quality of the loans is so poor that they will have to be sold at deep discounts, and second, once the loans are sold, the government loses a stream of interest receipts it would otherwise have received. Under the rules of budget accounting, the revenues from the loan sales are negative expenditures that reduce the reported deficit. In fact, however, from the standpoint of its impact on the economy, whether the federal government taps the private credit markets by issuing a government bond or by selling some of its own financial paper makes no difference at all. In either case the funds are withdrawn from the pool of private saving, leaving that much less to finance private investment.

The president also proposes to sell to private interests some of the government's "business" enterprises, the principal and most controversial of which are its power-producing and transmission facilities in the West. The president hopes, three to four years from now, to realize modest sums from these sales—$5 billion in 1990 and $13 billion over the five-year period 1987–91. But just as in the case of financial asset sales, the proceeds should not be counted toward reducing the deficit. Private parties will have to issue stocks and bonds and tap the private capital markets to buy these assets. Exactly the same amount of funds will be diverted from business investment in new plants and equipment whether the government finances its deficit by selling assets or by selling government bonds. While sales of assets, financial and real, may make the budget deficit look smaller and help meet the legal requirements of Gramm-Rudman-Hollings, they do not in fact reduce the damaging effects of the federal budget deficit on the availability of private saving to finance private business investment.

Do the sales of real and financial assets significantly affect future budget deficits and the subsequent operation of the federal government? In the case of financial assets the answer is clearly negative. When the government sells some of the loans or mort-gages that it holds to private investors, it can avoid selling some of its own Treasury securities; future interest payments on the national debt are lowered. But the stream of future interest receipts that the federal government gets from the loans it holds in its own portfolio is also reduced, and by approximately the same amount.[18] The impact of the federal government on the private sector is unchanged.

In the case of real federal assets the situation may be different. If the federal government were currently subsidizing a business-like operation—for example, selling electric power from the Bonneville Power Administration at rates below operating cost—sale of the assets to a private utility would end the future stream of subsidies. In fact, however, while the federal power adminis-trations all sell power at cut-rate prices—because their own costs are artificially low, thanks to low interest rates on long-term Treasury loans made years ago—there is no current federal subsidy being appropriated to these enterprises, and their sale to private industry would not significantly reduce the future cost of government. Nor would it be likely to net great present benefits. Since potential buyers will have to pay high real interest rates on the bonds they issue to finance their purchase, they will either have to raise the rates for electricity or pay the government a low purchase price.

Nevertheless, it would make economic sense to raise the electricity rate structure, gradually bringing it more nearly in line with the long-run economic cost of producing additional electricity in the region. Unfortunately, the same political opposition that now prevents the government from charging such rates will, in all likelihood, prevent it from achieving the same result by selling the power administrations to private industry.

Unlike many other countries the U.S. government does not own any major industries that currently receive large subsidies and whose sale to private enterprise would substantially reduce future budget costs. Still, it is reasonable for the government to assess whether any of its operations that resemble a business

18. If the loan held by the government is a subsidized loan paying market interest rates, the government will have to offer it at a discount to make it salable, so the outcome is as described above.

ought to be transferred to the private sector. Private industry, operating under the spur of the profit motive, might have incentives to run the operation more efficiently. Selling the operation off may be a way of ending unwarranted subsidies that are currently tied to government ownership. But these decisions should be made on a case-by-case basis. And they should not be undertaken simply to generate proceeds that can be used to lower the reported government deficit. As we have seen, such a decline in the deficit is apparent, not real. Disguising the true size of the deficit problem will ultimately do more harm than good.

4

Tax Policy Options

THE TAX SYSTEM suffers from two serious shortcomings. First, it raises too little revenue to pay for current government expenditures or even those likely to remain after any politically acceptable spending reductions. Chapter 3 shows that revenues should be increased $50 billion by 1989 to avoid indiscriminate cuts in defense and nondefense spending for purposes of deficit reduction.[1] Second, the tax system is unfair and induces inefficient economic behavior, in large measure because of the proliferation of special exclusions, deductions, credits, and allowances in personal and corporate income taxes. These special provisions, often introduced for meritorious reasons, have also reduced the revenue generated by any given set of tax rates.

For nearly one year Congress has been debating the merits of a tax reform plan submitted by President Reagan in May 1985.[2] This plan was designed expressly to deal with the second problem but not the first. It would broaden the base of both personal and corporate income taxes, but the additional revenues generated by these reforms would be used exclusively to reduce tax rates; none would be used to increase revenues. In December 1985 the House of Representatives passed a plan similar in many respects to the president's proposal.[3]

1. The administration proposes revenue increases totaling only $5.7 billion in fiscal year 1989. These increases are to come from two sources: higher excise taxes and increased contributions by federal employees to their retirement fund. If enacted, these increases would reduce the $50 billion revenue target correspondingly.

2. *The President's Tax Proposals to the Congress for Fairness, Growth, and Simplicity* (Government Printing Office, 1985).

3. H.R. 3838, Tax Reform Act of 1985.

Whatever the fate of this bill, total revenues will have to be increased if the targets of the Gramm-Rudman-Hollings law are to be met in a responsible way. To meet those targets, Congress should consider *both* tax reform *and* revenue increases in 1986. If, as we shall urge, tax reform deserves support, the question before Congress, the president, and the nation is how best to link reform with revenue increases. This chapter explores how this goal can be achieved.

Three broad alternatives present themselves. First, Congress can increase revenues by raising personal and corporation income taxes. The current effort to reform the income tax complicates this course, however. To boost revenues and to reform the income tax requires either modifications in the tax reform bill, so that it raises more revenues than are produced under current law, or completion of the tax reform legislation and then enactment of a separate bill to raise rates or broaden the tax base even more than had been done through reform. In either event tax rates lower than those under current law would suffice to meet the $50 billion revenue target if the tax base is broadened enough. For example, an increase of 2 percentage points in personal and corporation tax rates provided by the House bill would raise about $50 billion in fiscal year 1989, yet the individual income tax rate in the top bracket would be 10 percentage points lower than the present top rate (40 percent compared with 50 percent) and the general corporation rate would be 8 percentage points lower (38 percent instead of 46 percent).

The second way to raise additional revenues is by increasing excise taxes on selected consumer goods. The most obvious candidates are energy, alcoholic beverages, and tobacco products. We believe that selected excise taxes should be increased whether or not income tax reform succeeds.

Finally, Congress could raise additional revenues by imposing a broad-based tax on consumption—either a federal retail sales tax or a national value-added tax. Part of the revenues from a sales or value-added tax could be used to reduce personal and corporation income tax rates and part to increase revenues. Such a tax could be enacted whether the current tax reform effort succeeds or fails, but the administrative problems of introducing a new tax mean that it could not begin to generate revenues much before fiscal year 1989. Senator William V. Roth, Jr. (Republican of Delaware), has sponsored a type of value-added tax, which he calls a "business transfer tax." But all the revenue from this tax would be used to cut personal and corporation income taxes; none would be used to boost revenues.

This chapter considers the strengths and weaknesses of each of these approaches to raising revenues. We conclude that the first option is the most attractive. By combining reform of the personal and corporation income taxes with reductions in tax rates only slightly smaller than those proposed by the House, Congress can make the most important sources of revenue fairer and less distorting and can raise revenues in a timely fashion. Congress could also enact increases in some excise taxes to meet at least part of the revenue targets discussed in chapter 3. These taxes probably cannot raise enough revenue to avoid increases in other taxes as well (unless their rates are set disruptively high), but they could be used to hold down the size of the income tax increases necessary to meet the revenue targets. If it appears that income and excise taxes cannot be increased, perhaps because of presidential opposition, Congress will be forced to consider a broad-based tax on consumption. Any one of these methods of increasing revenues is preferable to a continuation of the deficits currently projected.

Tax Reform

The current system imposes widely unequal tax burdens on individuals and business enterprises with equal incomes and produces numerous distortions in the economy. Tax reform aims to broaden the tax base by eliminating unnecessary deductions, exclusions, and credits and uses the additional revenue to reduce tax rates. The elimination of tax preferences would mean that different sources of income would be taxed more equally than they now are and that economic distortions would be reduced. The reduction in marginal tax rates would promote work effort and saving. A simpler tax code would improve understanding of the tax laws and reduce the complexities of administration and compliance. The tax reform plan proposed by the administration and the House bill would move toward these objectives, although each deviates widely from the ideal of a comprehensive income tax reform.

The administration's tax reform plan, submitted to Congress in May 1985, had four central characteristics.

—The income level at which people become liable for income tax in 1986 was to be sharply increased by two measures. Personal exemptions were to be increased from $1,080 a person to $2,000 a person. The zero bracket amount (or standard deduction) was to be increased from $3,670 for married couples and $2,480 for single persons to $4,000 for married couples and $2,900 for single persons. As a result the taxable threshold would rise from $7,990 to $12,000 for families of four, and from $3,280 to $4,900 for single persons. These changes would restore the principle, followed through most of the 1970s, that family units with incomes below the officially defined poverty levels should not be required to pay income taxes.

—Marginal tax rates on both individuals and corporations would have been reduced sharply. The maximum marginal individual income tax rate would have fallen from 50 percent to 35 percent. The maximum marginal corporation tax rate would have fallen from 46 percent to 33 percent.

—The revenue loss from reductions in corporation and personal income tax rates would have been made up by numerous amendments to broaden the tax base. Of these changes, the most important one affecting corporations was the proposed repeal of the investment tax credit, which would increase revenues by $88 billion from 1987 through 1989. The most important expansion of the personal income tax base was the proposed repeal of deductibility for state and local taxes. Compared with current law, this change would have added $104 billion to revenues from 1987 through 1989.

—Tax collections from individuals would have been decreased; those on corporations would have been increased. In 1987–1989, corporate income tax payments would have risen by $82 billion and personal tax payments would have fallen by $88 billion.

The House followed the general outlines and affirmed many of the specific elements of the administration's proposal. It adhered to the principle that personal income tax collections should be cut and that corporation income tax collections should be increased. It proposed to cut personal income taxes and increase corporation income taxes by about the same amount as would have occurred under the administration bill. But the House also made a number of important changes.

—The House bill increases the personal exemption to $2,000 but reduces it by $500 a person if the taxpayer itemizes deductions. The standard deduction is raised to $4,800 for married couples and $2,950 for single persons. These changes would raise the taxable threshold to $12,800 for a family of four and $4,950 for individuals.

—The House accepts the idea that marginal tax rates should be cut, but the cuts are smaller for most taxpayers than those sought by the administration because it broadens the tax base less than the administration proposed. The top bracket rate would be reduced to 38 percent instead of 35 percent. (Table 4-1 compares the tax rates under current law, those in the House bill, and those proposed by the president.)[4]

—Like the administration, the House calls for the end of the investment tax credit but proposes less generous depreciation deductions than the administration suggested. The top corporation rate would be 36 percent rather than 33 percent.

—The House accepts many but by no means all the changes proposed by the administration to broaden the tax base. Among the more important proposals it does not accept is elimination of the deduction for state and local taxes.

---

4. The calculations in table 4-1 show the marginal tax rate, or the tax on additions to income, at each income level. Total taxes at each income level are not shown. In the case of a single taxpayer earning $20,000, the marginal tax rate increases from 23 percent under current law to 25 percent under the House bill, but total taxes decline from $2,258 to $2,139.

These calculations assume that taxpayers under current law claim itemized deductions equal to 23 percent of income or the zero bracket amount, whichever is greater. For the House bill and the president's proposal, itemized deductions are assumed to be 22 percent and 19.25 percent of income, respectively, reflecting the proposed changes in itemized deductions in each case. Married couples are assumed to have one earner. No account is taken here of the effects of the earned-income credit on marginal tax rates in lower-income households. For indexing exemption amounts and rate brackets under current law, an inflation rate of 3.5 percent between 1986 and 1987 is assumed.

Table 4-1. *Marginal Tax Rates under Present Law, the House Bill
(H.R. 3838), and the Administration's Proposal, 1987*
Percent unless otherwise indicated

Income (dollars)	Present law	House bill	Administration's proposal
Single persons			
10,000	15	15	15
20,000	23	25	15
30,000	26	25	25
50,000	38	35	25
100,000	48	38	35
200,000	50	38	35
Married couples with two children			
10,000	11	0	0
20,000	16	15	15
30,000	18	15	15
50,000	28	25	25
100,000	42	35	35
200,000	49	38	35

Source: Authors' calculations (see note 4 for assumptions underlying the calculations).

Tax reform legislation of this kind would improve the equity of the income tax by reducing the variation in effective tax rates imposed on households with similar incomes. It would eliminate some of the inefficiencies of the present system by reducing the differences among taxes imposed on various classes of investments and types of consumption. It would also have some effect on subsequent efforts to boost revenues. Proposals that have been explicitly considered and rejected are unlikely to be revived. The more that corporation taxes are increased to pay for individual tax cuts, the harder it will be to raise corporation taxes later. The fact that the proportion of federal revenues provided by the corporation income tax has fallen sharply—from 27 percent in 1955 to 17 percent in 1970 and to 8 percent in 1985—provided some justification for the president's initial proposals. However, the virtual cessation in growth of productivity since 1974 has dampened enthusiasm for increasing taxes like the corporation income tax that might discourage saving or investment.

Because Congress is considering income tax reform during the same year in which it may wish to increase revenues, it must decide whether to take these issues up jointly or separately. This chapter sets out three methods of raising revenues; clearly, however, two or more could be combined. They could also be linked to tax reform, either in a single bill or in two jointly negotiated but separately enacted bills; or they could be approached as if they were independent of tax reform.

Income Tax Options

The president's tax reform plan and the House bill each broaden the income tax base and lower rates, but neither would increase revenues during the next five years. Revenues could be raised by broadening the base even more, by reducing rates less, or by some combination of these steps.

Broadening the Base

Raising revenue by broadening the base of personal and corporation income taxes would require Congress to reconsider some changes that did not survive the debate on tax reform. Some reforms with a large potential for increasing revenues are politically unthinkable. Repealing the deduction for mortgage interest, for example, would increase federal revenue by about $24 billion in 1989, but President Reagan insisted on preserving this deduction in fashioning his tax plan, and Congress shows no inclination to curtail it.[5]

The chances for passage of other major reforms to broaden the tax base may be almost as remote. However, three reforms excluded from the House bill merit reconsideration: taxing at least part of fringe benefits provided by employers, taxing an increased

5. Any reform that reduces marginal tax rates curtails the value of all deductions and exclusions (the lower the tax rate, the smaller the reduction in taxes per dollar of deduction). And the increase in the zero bracket amount would cause many people who previously itemized to stop doing so. The $24 billion figure mentioned in the text and subsequent estimates are based on the lower tax rates and higher standard deductions in the tax bill passed by the House of Representatives in December 1985. Therefore the estimates are substantially lower—by one-quarter to one-third, depending on the provision—than comparable items in the tax expenditure estimates presented in "Special Analysis G" of the *Budget of the United States Government, Fiscal Year 1987.*

proportion of social security and railroad retirement benefits, and curtailing deductions for state and local taxes. These changes would reduce the growth of noncash compensation and improve tax equity among workers in essentially equal circumstances.

In November 1984 the Treasury Department urged that most fringe benefits provided by employers be considered taxable income.[6] These benefits currently provide disproportionate tax advantages to some taxpayers, encourage employers to substitute noncash for cash compensation, and increase tax rates necessary to raise a given amount of revenue. Under the Treasury plan, only contributions to qualified pension plans and up to $175 of health insurance a month for families ($70 a month for individuals) would not be taxed. This approach was a compromise between retaining open-ended tax incentives for employers to provide health insurance and discouraging the provision of generous benefits that contribute to increases in medical costs. Faced with the vehement opposition of the chairman of the Senate Finance Committee, the administration scrapped the Treasury approach and suggested instead that the first $25 a month of health insurance for families ($10 for individuals) should be included in taxable income, an approach that has no obvious rationale other than that it solved a political problem. Dan Rostenkowski (Democrat of Illinois), chairman of the House Committee on Ways and Means, then returned to the Treasury approach but proposed higher ceilings on the exclusion ($300 a month for families, $120 for single persons). The committee and the full House chose to retain the current complete exclusion.

Congress should also reconsider the tax treatment of social security and railroad retirement benefits, both of which closely resemble benefits provided by private pensions. Social security benefits were not taxed until 1984, when Congress decided to tax half the benefits received by married couples with incomes above $32,000 and single persons with incomes above $25,000. The rationale for taxing only half is that employee contributions, which account for half the total tax, are paid out of after-tax incomes. However, the high income thresholds are arbitrary and violate

6. See U.S. Department of the Treasury, *Tax Reform for Fairness, Simplicity, and Economic Growth,* 3 vols. (GPO, 1984).

Table 4-2. *Revenue Effects of Alternative Ways of Taxing Social Security and Fringe Benefits, Fiscal Years 1987–91*[a]
Billions of dollars

Benefits	1987	1988	1989	1990	1991
Social security benefits[b]					
Tax one-half of benefits, 50 percent lower thresholds (married $16,000; single $12,500)	1.1	3.9	4.1	4.3	4.6
Tax one-half of benefits, eliminate thresholds	1.9	6.5	6.8	7.2	7.6
Tax 90 percent of benefits, current thresholds	1.1	3.8	4.0	4.2	4.5
Tax 90 percent of benefits, 50 percent lower thresholds	3.4	11.6	12.2	12.8	13.6
Fringe benefits					
Tax employer-provided health premiums over $175 a month for families, $70 a month for individuals	2.9	4.8	5.8	7.2	8.8
Tax employer-provided health premiums over $300 a month for families, $120 a month for individuals	0.6	1.0	1.2	1.4	1.8
Tax employer-provided life insurance premiums	1.1	1.6	1.7	1.8	1.9

Sources: Congressional Budget Office; and authors' estimates.
a. Income tax effects only. Assumes effective date of January 1, 1987. Based on H.R. 3838.
b. Old age and survivors' benefits only.

the principle that people with equal incomes should pay the same tax. Applying the same tax rules to social security that are applied to private pensions would result in the inclusion in taxable income of about 90 percent of benefits with no threshold. With personal income tax thresholds near those in the House bill, people who rely entirely on social security benefits would pay little or no tax.

Table 4-2 shows the amounts of revenue that could be raised if Congress decided to tax part of fringe benefits or to increase the taxation of social security benefits. The revenue potential of such reforms is considerable, but so is the political opposition to them.

A more likely source of revenue is to limit the deductibility of state and local taxes. The administration proposed complete repeal of this deduction. Chairman Rostenkowski recommended

Table 4-3. *Revenue Effects of Alternative Limitations on Deductibility of State and Local Taxes, Fiscal Years 1987–91*[a]
Billions of dollars

Option	1987	1988	1989	1990	1991
Eliminate personal deduction for all state and local taxes	3.7	24.8	27.0	29.5	32.0
Eliminate personal deduction only for state and local sales and personal property taxes	0.6	3.6	4.0	4.4	4.8
Allow personal deduction only for state and local taxes over 1 percent of adjusted gross income	0.5	3.5	3.8	4.1	4.4
Allow personal deduction only for state and local taxes over 3 percent of adjusted gross income	1.5	10.5	11.4	12.4	13.4
Allow personal deduction only for state and local taxes over 5 percent of adjusted gross income	2.4	16.2	17.6	19.2	20.9

Sources: Congressional Budget Office; and authors' estimates.
a. Assumes effective date of January 1, 1987. Based on H.R. 3838.

reducing it, but the full Ways and Means Committee rejected any limitation, and the House ratified this decision. Even modest limits on the deductibility of state and local taxes could increase revenues significantly. For example, the deduction could be allowed only to the extent that state and local taxes exceed 1 percent, or 3 percent, or 5 percent of income. A strong case can also be made for outright repeal of the deduction of sales taxes. Most taxpayers do not calculate sales taxes paid. Instead they use Internal Revenue Service tables that are based only on income and state of residence. In effect, the sales tax deduction is a standard deduction and does not reflect the amount of taxes each individual pays. Based on the House bill, table 4-3 shows the amounts of revenue that could be raised by various combinations of these changes in the deduction for state and local taxes.

Yet another approach, embodied in the tax reform plan submitted by Senator Bill Bradley (Democrat of New Jersey) and Congressman Richard A. Gephardt (Democrat of Missouri), would

Table 4-4. *Revenue Effects of Alternative Income Tax Rate Increases, Fiscal Years 1987–91*[a]
Billions of dollars

Type of increase	1987	1988	1989	1990	1991
9 percent surtax on all individual and corporate taxpayers	32.4	46.3	50.9	55.6	60.8
2 percentage point rate increase on all individual and corporate taxpayers	33.2	47.7	52.4	57.0	62.1
10 percent rate increase on individuals, 5 percent on corporations	32.8	47.0	51.8	56.3	61.3

Sources: Brookings tax model; and Congressional Budget Office.
a. Assumes effective date of January 1, 1987. Based on H.R. 3838.

allow taxpayers to claim full deductions but only against tax rates up to some maximum.[7] Applying this approach to the tax rates proposed in the House bill would allow deductions to be claimed only against the 15 percent or 25 percent bracket. This approach preserves the full deduction for taxpayers whose marginal tax rate is no higher than the chosen maximum but curtails it for taxpayers subject to higher rates.

Raising Rates

The simplest way to boost income tax collections is to raise rates. If rate increases are joined to a tax reform plan like that proposed by the president or passed by the House, *marginal* tax rates would be higher than those contained in each of these proposals but would be below those in current law.

Here is why. The House bill broadens the tax base enough so that substantially lower rates yield as much revenue as current rates do. Under the House bill personal and corporate income taxes are projected to yield $565 billion in 1989. Thus an increase of slightly less than 9 percent of the tax liabilities of all taxpayers, individual and corporate, would increase revenues by $50 billion (see table 4-4). Alternatively, individual income taxes could be increased by 10 percent and corporation income taxes by 5 percent.

7. S. 409 and H.R. 800, Fair Tax Act of 1985.

Table 4-5. *Distribution of an Individual Tax Rate Increase*
of 10 Percent and an Increase of 2 Percentage Points
in Each Rate Bracket, by Income Bracket, 1986[a]

Adjusted gross income (dollars)	10 percent rate increase		2 percentage point rate increase	
	Millions of dollars	Percent of total	Millions of dollars	Percent of total
0– 5,000	23	*	23	*
5,000– 10,000	396	1.2	519	1.5
10,000– 15,000	1,132	3.4	1,473	4.4
15,000– 20,000	1,711	5.1	2,215	6.6
20,000– 30,000	4,396	13.0	5,326	15.9
30,000– 50,000	10,474	31.1	11,665	34.8
50,000–100,000	8,689	25.8	7,788	23.2
100,000–200,000	3,123	9.3	2,151	6.4
Over 200,000	3,745	11.1	2,387	7.1
Total	33,689	100.0	33,547	100.0

Source: Brookings tax model.
* Less than 0.05 percent.
a. Based on H.R. 3838, when fully phased in.

For individual taxpayers any pattern of rate changes is imaginable but two methods stand out as simplest—an equal *percentage* increase of 10 percent in all rates or an equal *absolute* increase of 2 percentage points in all rates (see table 4-5).[8] In each case, if the bill passed by the House in December 1985 is the starting point, marginal rates would remain below those in current law. The major difference between these two approaches is that a 10 percent increase in all tax rates would collect more of the additional revenue from high-income taxpayers and less from low-income taxpayers than would a 2 percentage point increase in the rates in every bracket (see table 4-5). Both methods would be progressive.

If revenues are to be increased, a strong case can be made for increasing income taxes. They are the only taxes tailored to the economic circumstances of each taxpaying unit. They are imposed at rates graduated to reflect social judgments about ability to pay.

8. These two forms of rate increases would raise the same amount of revenue from *individual* taxpayers. As noted above, to raise $50 billion in fiscal year 1989, rate increases of equivalent yield applied to *all* taxpayers—corporations and individuals— would be a 9 percent increase or a 2 percentage point increase in all rates.

All other major taxes would impose sizable burdens on households now regarded as too poor to pay income taxes and would impose proportionately smaller burdens on upper-income groups than on low- and middle-income groups. Successful tax reform can make personal and corporation income taxes fairer and more conducive to economic efficiency than they have been in the past.

Politics of Raising Income Tax Revenues

If Congress decides to increase income taxes, it will also have to decide whether to combine revenue-raising legislation with tax reform legislation or to enact two separate measures. Good political arguments can be made for and against each approach. But decisions on tax reform and tax increases will nevertheless be made at about the same time in 1986. If income taxes become the instrument of choice for increasing revenues, the best approach would be to have the broadest possible base and lowest possible rates as the starting point, whether these changes are embodied in one bill or two.

The major argument on behalf of separate bills is that the president adamantly opposes combining tax reform with revenue increases; legislation combining them would probably be vetoed. Moreover, a major attraction of tax reform is that most taxpayers will pay less individual income tax. Toward this end the president and the House shifted tax collections from individuals to corporations. The president has also touted the income tax portion of his reform plan as "tax reduction" because most households would face reduced liabilities and because households in general would pay less than they now do. Trying to combine reform with tax increases would undercut this appeal by increasing the number of individual taxpayers who would pay more tax and reducing the number who would pay less.[9]

9. Even if the individual income tax were called on to yield as much revenue as it does under current law, the gainers would outnumber the losers. Losers typically would be taxpayers who are denied particularly valuable itemized deductions, credits, or allowances and who would experience large tax increases. The gainers, in contrast, would tend to be taxpayers who do not itemize their deductions, a group that includes over 60 percent of all taxpayers, and who would benefit from reduced marginal tax rates, increased personal exemptions, and the increased standard deduction. Shifting taxes from individuals to corporations, as would occur under both the administration proposal and the House bill, would increase still further the percentage of gainers.

However, it may become politically impossible for members of Congress to support increases in income taxes for several years after tax reform is enacted. Having explicitly rejected some major measures to broaden the tax base, they would find it difficult or impossible to reverse themselves. And having just used the appeal of promised reductions in marginal tax rates to justify expanding the tax base, they would find it difficult to vote for increases in rates. The fact that marginal rates after both reform *and* tax increases would remain below those in current law would not deter opponents from portraying any tax increase as a betrayal of promises made to secure tax reform. These arguments suggest that tax reform and tax increases should be combined in a single bill, even in the face of a veto threat.

Some members of Congress advocate a "tax amnesty" as a way to boost revenues without raising rates or broadening the tax base. Under an amnesty, penalties and fines are forgiven in return for full payment of overdue taxes during some limited time period, perhaps three to six months. Massachusetts, New York, and a number of other states have used amnesties to collect overdue tax liabilities. The keys to a successful amnesty are a strong enforcement program after the amnesty ends and a credible promise that the amnesty will not be repeated. However, an amnesty also carries considerable risks. Some taxpayers may increase evasion in the hope that the amnesty will be repeated. Experience in other countries suggests that amnesties are in fact repeated, with considerable damage to taxpayer morale. Moreover, the one-time increase in revenue during the amnesty period does not make a permanent contribution to closing the deficit.

Rather than authorizing an amnesty, Congress should provide sufficient resources to the Internal Revenue Service to field a vigorous audit and enforcement program. Increases in IRS staff to support more vigorous efforts to prevent tax evasion have been proposed by the administration in its 1987 budget. Such efforts would generate additional revenues several times greater than the added administrative cost. But the Gramm-Rudman-Hollings law will force cuts in the IRS budget if the automatic provisions take effect. In the name of cutting the deficit this spending reduction would increase the deficit because the Internal Revenue Service would have fewer resources to find and prosecute tax evaders.

Selected Excise Taxes

Revenues from excise taxes on petroleum, alcoholic beverages, and tobacco account for only about 5 percent of federal receipts, but increasing these taxes could make a prompt, if modest, contribution to reducing the deficit. As additional advantages, higher energy taxes would promote energy conservation, and higher taxes on alcoholic beverages or tobacco products could have significant health benefits. Collections in fiscal year 1986 will amount to $11.3 billion from taxes on gasoline and diesel fuel and $4.2 billion from a "windfall" tax on the extraction of petroleum.[10] A tax of sixteen cents a pack on cigarettes and a variety of different taxes on other tobacco products, wine, beer, and spirits now yield over $10 billion a year.

Much the most important potential revenue source is energy. Taxes could be imposed on all domestically consumed energy or on imported energy only. Alternatively, additional taxes could be imposed only on petroleum products or, still more narrowly, on gasoline alone.

Each of these taxes would not only raise revenue but also advance other objectives. Taxes on imported petroleum products, for example, would discourage imports and thus reduce short-run dependency on foreign supplies. Such taxes would boost domestic prices, thereby producing several effects. Domestic producers would enjoy large windfall gains from increased prices on oil they were already producing. Increased prices would encourage households and businesses to conserve energy. Consumption of domestically produced petroleum products, however, would increase. The short-run reduction in U.S. dependence on foreign suppliers would result in greater future dependence because domestic resources would be depleted more rapidly. A tax on

10. The windfall profits tax is an excise tax on the difference between the current price of oil and a base price, depending on the type of oil produced. The tax is 70 percent for oil discovered before 1978 ("first-tier" oil), 60 percent for stripper oil or production from a national petroleum reserve ("second-tier" oil), and 30 percent for oil discovered in 1978 or later years. The tax is scheduled to phase out over a period of thirty-three months beginning in January 1988, or when cumulative revenues reach $227.3 billion, whichever is later. Revenues from the windfall profit tax reached a peak of $23.3 billion in fiscal year 1981, but they have declined sharply as oil prices have declined. Receipts from the windfall profits tax are now estimated at $2.8 billion in 1987.

Table 4-6. *Revenue Effects of Increases in Energy Taxes,*
Fiscal Years 1987–91
Billions of dollars

Tax[a]	1987	1988	1989	1990	1991
Oil import fee of $5 a barrel	7.4	7.3	7.4	7.8	7.9
Excise tax on domestic and imported oil of $5 a barrel	20.4	21.8	22.1	22.5	22.9
Increase motor fuel excise tax by 30 cents a gallon	25.6	25.6	25.6	25.2	24.9
Broad-based tax on domestic energy consumption of 10 percent of value	25.0	26.6	27.5	28.5	29.6

Sources: Congressional Budget Office; and authors' estimates.
a. Assumes increases would be effective October 1, 1986.

imported petroleum would generate revenues from two sources.
The first would be the imports themselves (although at a reduced
level). The second would be domestic production, because the
rise in the price of domestic petroleum products would increase
revenues from the windfall profits tax. An import tax of $5 a barrel
would increase revenues by $7.4 billion in 1989 (see table 4-6).
This estimate assumes that oil imports from all sources would be
subject to tax. If exemptions were provided for imports from some
countries, such as Canada or Mexico, considerably less revenue
would be produced, especially as imports shifted to exempted
countries. The increase in domestic oil prices would be substantially reduced as well.

Taxes on both domestically produced petroleum and imported
petroleum would reduce consumption of petroleum products and
imports but would not accelerate the depletion of domestic reserves. A general oil tax levied at the rate of $5 a barrel would
raise about $22 billion in 1989 (see table 4-6). Such a tax would
raise more revenues at lower rates than an import tax alone. All
the revenues from the domestic price increase would go to the
federal treasury, but under the import tax alone, two-thirds of the
revenues from higher oil prices would go to domestic producers
as higher profits. World oil prices have now fallen to such an
extent that even an excise tax of $5 a barrel would leave the price
of petroleum inclusive of tax well below the 1981 price of $35 a
barrel.

These taxes suffer from important shortcomings, however. Both would directly increase prices, and additional inflationary effects could be expected as wages adjusted to these higher prices. Both would place the heaviest burdens on low-income taxpayers, who spend a relatively high percentage of their income on energy. The taxes would also encourage consumers of all kinds to substitute other forms of energy for petroleum, even if these alternative sources were more costly to produce. Such substitutions reduce economic efficiency. Both taxes would increase prices for all users of petroleum products, regardless of the importance of those uses. Finally, the burden of both taxes would differ widely in different parts of the country.

Because of these objections, an increase in the tax on gasoline might be considered instead. Gasoline taxes in the United States are low compared with those in other countries. An increase would promote energy conservation at low cost in compliance and administration. A tax of thirty cents a gallon would meet half the $50 billion revenue target. However, such a tax would also place burdens on people of limited means who must drive long distances or who lack access to mass transportation. As with other excise taxes, an increase in the gasoline tax would raise the consumer price index.

A tax of 10 percent on the value of all domestically produced energy would generate $27.5 billion in 1989. It would discourage consumption of energy of all kinds, even coal, which the United States has in sufficient quantity to consume at current levels for several hundred years. It would also increase prices, precipitating demands for higher wages.

A review of this list of possible taxes on petroleum and other sources of energy, domestic or imported, suggests that it would be technically possible to meet the $50 billion revenue targets by approximately doubling the tax rates shown in table 4-6. Doing so, however, would produce unacceptable disruptions. It would be possible to raise $7.5 billion to $25 billion a year from these taxes without serious consequences, but other revenues would still have to be found to meet the $50 billion target.

Revenues from additional excise taxes on tobacco and alcoholic beverages would reduce but still not eliminate the revenue problem. Doubling taxes on these products would, however, add

Table 4-7. *Revenue Effects of Increases in Cigarette and Alcohol Excise Taxes, Fiscal Years 1987–91*
Billions of dollars

Tax[a]	1987	1988	1989	1990	1991
Increase cigarette tax to					
32 cents a pack[b]	3.5	5.1	5.1	5.1	5.1
Double tax on distilled spirits					
to $25.00 a proof gallon	2.4	3.3	3.3	3.3	3.3
Double tax on beer and wine	0.9	1.1	1.2	1.2	1.2
Increase tax on beer and wine					
to current rate for distilled spirits	5.7	6.2	6.3	6.4	6.5

Source: Congressional Budget Office; and authors' estimates.
a. Assumes increase would be effective October 1, 1986.
b. Assumes scheduled reduction of cigarette tax from 16 cents to 8 cents a pack on March 15, 1986.

another $9.6 billion a year to revenues in 1989 (see table 4-7).[11] This step would also help to reduce consumption of these harmful products and require those who continue to consume them to pay at least part of the costs they impose on society.

Additional excise taxes could increase revenues $15 billion to $30 billion in 1989 and contribute significantly to meeting the revenue targets set forth in chapter 3. But they cannot relieve Congress of the necessity of raising other taxes as well if the Gramm-Rudman-Hollings targets are to be met without devastating effects on defense or nondefense programs.

Broad-Based Taxes on Consumption

Numerous economists and members of Congress have argued that the United States should raise more of its revenues from a broad-based consumption tax such as a national retail sales tax or a value-added tax.[12] They argue that by taxing capital income the

11. The revenue estimates assume doubling the cigarette tax at the level it was before March 15, 1986, when eight cents of the tax was scheduled to expire.
12. We do not discuss here the possibility of restructuring the entire income tax system along the lines of a cash-flow tax, which would be based on expenditures (including gifts and bequests) rather than income. Such a tax has the merit that it would not bias the tax system toward current consumption and against saving, as present law does. It could also be progressive in incidence, in contrast to a value-added tax. However, we believe that such a tax should not be adopted as a supplemental revenue source to raise the modest amounts of revenue required in the next several years. For

income tax discourages saving. They also hold that a national sales tax or value-added tax would be relatively easy to administer. Some have argued that it is fairer to base taxes on consumption, a measure of the use of resources, than to base them on income, a measure of the contribution to resources. In addition, developed countries in Europe and several large developing nations impose value-added taxes that are rebated on exports and imposed on imports. Some advocates of value-added taxation maintain that U.S. companies could compete more effectively against foreign firms if the United States instituted such a value-added tax to replace income taxes on both businesses and individuals, which cannot be rebated on exports or imposed on imports.

The most obvious and undeniable strength of broad-based taxes on consumption is that they yield a great deal of revenue even at low rates. In 1989 each percentage point of tax on the sales of all consumption goods would yield an estimated $21 billion; if food, housing and medical care were exempt, the yield would amount to $12.5 billion.[13]

In practice, retail sales taxes or value-added taxes are not imposed on a comprehensive tax base. The difficulty of measuring certain types of retail sales or value-added taxes leads to the exemption of some transactions;[14] the desire to reduce the regressivity of either tax by exempting essentials or taxing them at lower rates leads to further narrowing of the base of such taxes.[15] As a

---

detailed discussion of the cash-flow tax, see Alice M. Rivlin, ed., *Economic Choices 1984* (Brookings, 1984), pp. 87–118; and Henry J. Aaron and Harvey Galper, *Assessing Tax Reform* (Brookings, 1985), pp. 66–107.

13. These figures are based on estimates by the Congressional Budget Office. The retail sales tax base ordinarily excludes sales to businesses and sales of investment goods to households. The value-added tax base ordinarily equals the gross receipts of businesses, less purchases from other firms. The value-added tax may be calculated in a variety of ways: by imposing a tax on a firm's gross sales and allowing a rebate for all taxes previously paid by the firm's suppliers (the "invoice" method); by imposing a tax on the sum of all payments to labor through wages and salaries and to capital through profits, interest, rents, and royalties (the "addition" method); or by imposing a tax on each company based on the difference between its gross receipts and its payments to other companies (the "subtraction" method). In Europe the invoice method is used almost exclusively. See Congressional Budget Office, *Reducing the Deficit: Spending and Revenue Options* (GPO, 1986), p. 228.

14. The housing services consumed by owner-occupants, for example, should be included in retail sales, and these services generate some value added. As a practical matter, such "sales" or value added cannot be taxed.

15. The item most usually exempted for this reason is food, although some jurisdictions exempt other items such as transportation, prescription drugs, children's clothing, and other essentials.

result of such exemptions the base of a practical national retail sales or value-added tax would be about 40 percent smaller than a comprehensive base. Accordingly, to meet the revenue target of $50 billion set forth in chapter 3, the tax rate would have to be a least 4 percent rather than the 2.5 percent rate implied by a comprehensive base.

Alternatively, Congress might set a higher rate, reduce the deficit with part of the revenue, and use the rest to pay either for reductions in other taxes or for selective increases in expenditures. Senator William V. Roth, Jr., for example, has proposed a value-added tax of 7 percent to 10 percent, all of the revenue from which would be used to replace revenues lost from reductions in personal and corporate income tax rates, liberalized depreciation deductions, and increases in the limits on tax-free deposits into individual retirement accounts (to $10,000 a person each year). The Roth plan is intended to be revenue neutral, but with higher rates or less generous reductions in income taxes it could generate sufficient revenues to make a major contribution to reducing the deficit.

Unfortunately the Roth plan, like all other value-added taxes and retail sales taxes, could not help much in closing the deficit until 1989.[16] Problems of implementing a new tax would prevent any revenue from being collected by either tax during 1987 and much or all of 1988, if European experience with the value-added tax is any guide. Even European countries that replaced administratively similar taxes with value-added taxes allowed about two years from the time the new tax was enacted until revenues began to flow.[17]

Other taxes would have to be imposed during 1987 and 1988 if the targets of the Gramm-Rudman-Hollings law are to be met.

16. The Roth "business transfer tax" proposal (S. 1102) suffers from another shortcoming. The draft proposal calls for a value-added tax administered according to the "subtraction" method. This method would permit imports to be fully taxed, but it would be hard to rebate precisely all value-added taxes on exports. The problem arises because there is no way for the tax authorities to know how much tax was actually paid at earlier stages of production unless all industries are taxed identically. If, as is more common, different industries are taxed at different rates and some industries are entirely exempt, the computation of taxes actually paid on exported goods would be extremely cumbersome. Taxes paid at earlier stages of production would have to be approximated.

17. See Henry J. Aaron, ed., *The Value-Added Tax: Lessons from Europe* (Brookings, 1981).

Such taxes could include temporary income tax surcharges or temporary or permanent selective excise taxes. As value-added taxes began to flow, the revenues could be used to phase out the temporary taxes or to reduce other taxes.

A value-added or retail sales tax would fall on low-income and moderate-income households who are or would be excused from any income tax liability. Even exempting food and other necessities from taxation would not eliminate this problem. Families of four with incomes of up to $12,800, for example, would not be required to pay income tax under the House tax reform plan but would pay value-added or sales taxes on taxable consumption items. A variety of instruments could be used to attenuate this problem. Transfer payments, such as food stamps or public assistance, could be liberalized. Personal exemptions could be made refundable at some tax rate if the taxpayer has too little income to pay income taxes. Or family allowances could be introduced. But these "solutions" to the regressivity of broad-based consumption taxes would add considerable administrative complexity to a tax that is intended to be relatively simple. And they all cost money, thereby increasing the rate that would have to be imposed to reach any given net revenue target.

A national value-added or retail sales tax would also be strongly resisted by the states, which have traditionally regarded broad-based sales taxes as their exclusive revenue domain. At a time when federal budget cutbacks are putting additional pressure on state budgets, they would be extremely reluctant to share this revenue source.

The introduction of a value-added or retail sales tax would also tend to boost prices. Neither would apply to exports; a retail sales tax is not imposed on exports and a value-added tax would be rebated. But both would add to the prices paid by consumers. The extent to which such an increase in consumer prices would encourage a wage-price spiral is, however, uncertain. Clearly, if workers obtained full compensation for the initial price increase, wages would rise and prices would eventually increase by a multiple of the initial effect. But in the context of other background events, such as falling oil prices and increases in the prices of other imports because of the depreciation of the dollar, the ultimate effects on prices from the introduction of a value-added tax would be hard to assess. In any event the total increase would probably be modest because $50 billion is just under 1 percent of GNP in 1989.

Introducing a value-added or retail sales tax is thus decidedly second-best to increasing income taxes as a way to help reduce the deficit. Such consumption taxes cannot begin to generate revenues for approximately two years. They are more likely than are income tax increases to trigger inflation. They will require a new layer of administration and a new staff to administer them. And they impose taxes on people who are excused from other taxes.

But broad-based consumption taxes have major advantages as well. They raise a lot of revenue at low rates. They will fall on some taxpayers who avoid most or all income taxes but who cannot avoid consuming. They can be adjusted flexibly as revenue requirements fluctuate, without necessitating disruptive changes in take-home pay that alterations in income taxes generate. And they would permit lower tax burdens on the small share of capital income that is fully taxed each year. If an agreement to boost income and excise taxes proves elusive, the introduction of a value-added or retail sales tax is the only other way to raise substantial revenues to help reduce the deficit.

Fiscal Implications of Alternative Taxes

Increasing revenues and thereby reducing the deficit will produce important macroeconomic benefits, as indicated in chapter 2. Reducing the deficit by increasing any of the taxes described in this chapter will promote national saving, lead to an increase in investment, and reduce the foreign trade imbalance if monetary policies are eased as the deficit is reduced. Any differences in the effects of the various taxes described in this chapter would be small in comparison with the results of lowering the deficit. Increasing the income tax is likely to have similar macroeconomic effects whatever the source of additional revenues. Whether the base were broadened by reducing the deduction for state and local taxes, by taxing currently excluded fringe benefits or transfer payments, or in other ways, or whether tax rates were increased, the economic effects would differ little from those flowing from cuts in public spending along the lines sketched in chapter 3.

The other taxes—selective excise taxes or a broad-based consumption tax—might have some additional important, if second-order, macroeconomic effects. Each would boost prices, encouraging demands for higher wages and adding somewhat to inflation. Each would also have effects on international trade or domestic investment in addition to those attributable to changes in the deficit. Replacing taxes on capital income with a broad-based consumption tax would tend to increase the after-tax rate of return in the United States and might induce some increase in domestic saving. To the extent that U.S. taxes fall on foreigners, such reductions would tend to increase the flow of capital to the United States from abroad and cause some appreciation of the U.S. dollar relative to foreign currencies. This development would reduce the competitiveness of U.S. exports or of U.S. goods that compete with imports.

A Recommended Program

Tax increases will have to be part of any politically acceptable and economically defensible program of meeting the deficit reduction targets of the Gramm-Rudman-Hollings legislation. Our first choice is to increase personal and corporation income taxes. This could be instituted promptly and with few inflationary effects. If combined with or planned in conjunction with tax reform, such tax increases can be distributed equitably and can reduce distortions in economic behavior at the same time.

Consideration should also be given to increasing selected excise taxes. These taxes would promote other objectives as well as increased revenues. A tax on oil or gasoline would encourage conservation, and higher taxes on alcoholic beverages and tobacco products would reduce consumption of products that cause illness and increase demands for costly public and private services.

The last choice would be a broad-based consumption tax. Such a tax is capable of meeting the revenue targets in 1989, but because of delays in introducing it, the 1987 and 1988 targets could not be met. The consumption tax would have to be joined to other permanent or temporary revenue increases—for example, a temporary income tax surcharge or permanent increases in selected excise taxes.

Our central conclusion, however, is that the universal and legitimate aversion to paying taxes should not prevent the inclusion of revenue-raising measures in any program to reduce the deficit.

5

Improving the Budget Process

AT THE END of his 1986 State of the Union address, President Reagan described the budget process as "broken" and invited Speaker of the House Thomas P. (Tip) O'Neil to help him fix it. The process by which the U.S. government arrives at a budget is complicated and arcane, and it is hard to find anyone who likes it. The process consumes enormous amounts of executive branch and congressional time and energy, but the decisions are hardly ever finished. Deadlines are missed, and government agencies frequently run on "continuing resolutions" rather than regular appropriations. Occasionally a president makes a show of closing down the government for a few hours because agreement has not been reached on further funding.

Worst of all, for the past five years the result of this increasingly agonizing process has been massive budget deficits that none of the participants profess to want. Frustrated with the continuing deficits and their inability to reduce them, Congress and the president agreed in the fall of 1985 on the Gramm-Rudman-Hollings law. The law was enacted in desperation to break the deadlock between Congress and the president and reduce the deficit, but not even its staunchest defenders regard it as a desirable process for making a budget. Whether or not this desperate gamble will work to reduce the deficit, the question remains: what can be done to improve the budget process?

A drastic simplification of the process is in order. Decisions should be made less often. Most spending decisions should be made for two or more years at a time, and possibly the whole budget should be shifted to a biennial basis. Congressional committees should be restructured and the authorization and appropriation functions combined. The budget itself should be simplified and the number of line items greatly reduced, actions that would help shift congressional attention toward major policy issues and away from detailed micromanagement. As for the Gramm-Rudman-Hollings law, we share the hope that it will hasten agreement on deficit reduction but we regard it as a bad budget process. Constraining the budget deficit to a particular number—whether by law or constitutional amendment—risks destabilizing the economy.

Making the budget process simpler and more comprehensible, however, would not make the decisions easier. Budget making is inherently difficult for any organization, whether it be a family, a business, a university, or a government. There are never enough resources to carry out all desired activities. Choices have to be made, and these choices often bring to the surface deeply divergent views about the organization's purpose, how that purpose should be carried out, and who should bear the burdens or reap the benefits.

The Constitution deliberately divides budget power between the president and Congress and between the House and the Senate. The president can propose changes in budgetary priorities, but the ultimate power to levy taxes and authorize spending public funds is lodged in Congress, subject only to presidential veto. This divided power works well when the president and Congress are in broad agreement or are able to compromise their differences. It leads to deadlock and frustration when congressional and presidential views differ and one or both are unwilling to strike a bargain. Recent deficits have reflected the collision between the president's opposition to increasing taxes or reducing defense growth and the unwillingness of Congress to cut domestic spending by the amounts or in the ways proposed by the president.

Different congressional or executive branch procedures would not have resolved this political conflict. Short of a fundamental alteration of the constitutional separation of powers—which we doubt is either feasible or desirable—major differences on budget policy between the president and Congress can be resolved only by strong leadership combined with a willingness to compromise.

Evolution of the Budget Process

Surprisingly, despite all the talk about the budget and the budget process, no budget for the U.S. government is ever actually enacted as such. Government spending and revenue in any one year result from the application of a large number of separate laws passed at different times that specify the revenue raising and spending powers of the government. The elaborate set of documents labeled *The Budget of the United States Government,* which the president issues with such fanfare each year, contains a large number of proposals, detailed estimates of what will be spent and collected in the next year if the president's recommendations for spending and taxing laws are accepted by Congress and the economy behaves as the administration assumes (or hopes) it will.

Because of the separation of powers, the history of budget making in the U.S. government is two separate histories: that of executive branch efforts to evolve a procedure for crafting the president's budget proposals and that of congressional efforts to make spending and taxing decisions in a more orderly way. Gramm-Rudman-Hollings is unique because it tries for the first time to deal with the efforts simultaneously and create a procedure for forcing the president and Congress to attain an agreed budget deficit target *together.* It is not yet clear whether this objective can be achieved in a way that does not violate the constitutional separation of powers.

Evolution of the Presidential Process

The U.S. government had no budget decision process at all until after World War I. Throughout the nineteenth and early twentieth centuries, the central government had few budget responsibilities, and government agencies took their requests for funds directly to Congress. The president had no formal process for reviewing or constraining these agency requests.

The Budget and Accounting Act of 1921 represented a major departure from these practices: it was the first in a series of institutional changes designed to make sure the president controlled requests for funds and proposed a budget that reflected the views and priorities of his administration. The act created a new staff, now called the Office of Management and Budget, charged with examining the requests of agencies and providing the president with the information on which to base budget proposals. Subsequently, the Employment Act of 1946 charged the newly created Council of Economic Advisers with responsibility for forecasting economic developments, assisting the president in formulating fiscal policy, and making an annual economic report to Congress. The 1960s and 1970s saw a series of attempts in the executive branch to improve the systematic evaluation of government programs, to look further into the future at needs for government action, to estimate the costs, benefits, and distributional effects of alternative spending or taxing programs, and to organize the process of budget decisionmaking on a firm schedule.

Thus by the early 1970s the executive branch of the government had institutionalized budget making. The president was well equipped to translate his political predilections into budget proposals. But the result of all this executive activity was just a set of proposals. Congress had the responsibility for making the ultimate budget decisions.

Evolution of the Congressional Process

Unlike the executive branch, by the 1970s Congress had evolved no comparably centralized institutions. Before 1974 no committee had legislative responsibility for budget policy as a whole. Many spending decisions were made in two stages. First, authorizing committees worked on bills authorizing spending for particular programs. Even if such bills were passed by both houses and signed by the president, no money could be spent until a separate appropriations bill made its way through another set of committees in both houses and was approved and signed into law. More than a dozen major appropriations bills were voted on at different times of the year. Relative priorities, such as defense as opposed to education or health, were never explicitly considered.

Spending for social insurance and other entitlement programs, which was growing rapidly in the 1960s and 1970s, remained outside the normal appropriations process. Amounts spent on these programs were determined automatically once the characteristics of beneficiaries and the level of their benefits were defined by legislation.

Revenue bills came out of different committees and were voted on separately from spending measures. Because the spending and taxing sides were never brought together, there was no moment at which Congress voted on the question of whether revenues and expenditures were in appropriate relationship to each other. Congressional budget policy was the accidental result of spending and revenue decisions influenced by different committees and made at different times.

Spurred by feelings of frustration and impotence in confronting President Nixon, whose priorities differed from their own, members of Congress finally took a long overdue step and passed the Congressional Budget Act of 1974. The act created budget committees in each house charged with formulating an overall budget policy that, when passed by Congress in the form of a budget resolution, would serve as a controlling framework within which individual taxing and spending measures could be fitted.

The Congressional Budget Act provided for an elaborate three-stage budget process spread over a nine-month period between January, when the president's budget proposal was made, and October 1, when the new fiscal year began. In the first stage the budget committees would produce a first concurrent resolution on the budget that would specify the aggregate level of federal spending for the next year, break down that spending by major categories (but not by detailed line items), and indicate revenues to be available and the resulting deficit or surplus. After this resolution was agreed upon, specific appropriations and tax bills would be passed in line with the aggregate numbers specified in the resolution. These, however, were regarded as targets and were not absolutely binding. In the final stage Congress would reconsider whether the targets in the first resolution were still appropriate and, if necessary, reconcile specific bills with the desired aggregates. A second concurrent resolution on the budget— this time a binding one—would then be passed.

The Congressional Budget Act gave Congress a much needed mechanism for making overall budget decisions. Unfortunately, however, it also made an already complex and lengthy decision process still more complicated and time consuming. The new process retained all the existing authorizing, appropriating, and tax writing committees and added yet another layer: the budget committees. The resulting schedule of detailed and difficult decisions to be made in sequence each year was impossibly demanding, even if reasonable agreement existed on overall budget policy.

For example, it soon became apparent that two budget resolutions were too many. The compromises on budget priorities needed to pass a first budget resolution were difficult to achieve and often occurred later than the May 15 deadline. Once an agreement was achieved, no one wanted to reopen the arguments. Hence the second resolution quickly became a formality, then was officially folded into the first.

The new decision process established by the Congressional Budget Act of 1974 accomplished its major purpose. It gave Congress a forum for deciding fiscal policy. In the stagflation of the 1970s, for example, the fiscal choices were agonizing. The desirability of stimulating the economy and reducing unemployment had to be weighed against the danger of aggravating already high levels of inflation. In the deep recession of 1975—the first year of the new process—Congress used the budget resolution to approve a larger fiscal stimulus than originally proposed by President Ford. Later in the decade Congress, reflecting mounting popular concern with inflation, tended to moderate the fiscal stimulus proposed by the Carter administration.

In 1981 President Reagan, fresh from a massive electoral victory, used the centralized features of the budget process effectively to obtain congressional approval of drastic changes in the federal budget. The major elements of the Reagan program—tax cuts, increases in defense spending, and reductions in domestic spending—were embodied in a three-year budget resolution and passed by Congress as a package.

Reconciliation, the process originally associated with the second budget resolution, was used to bring entitlement programs and other ongoing spending legislation into conformity with the reduced domestic spending totals in the first (and only) budget resolution. These numerous, complex, and sometimes far-reaching changes in existing laws were also voted as a single package.

The events of 1981 showed that a president with strong views on budget priorities and a recent election mandate could use the congressional budget process to obtain rapid ratification of dramatic changes in the budget as a whole. The fragmented decision process that existed before the 1974 reforms would have made these instant, simultaneous changes in many parts of the budget much less feasible. President Reagan's use of the reconciliation process for wholesale alteration of detailed spending legislation, however, left many congressional committees, especially in the Democratic House of Representatives, bruised and determined to reassert their traditional powers.

The budget decisions made in 1981 resulted in enormous deficits in subsequent years. The tax cuts reduced federal revenues as a percent of GNP while spending continued to increase. The future deficits were not anticipated in 1981, in part because the budget resolution assumed unspecified future cuts in domestic spending that never materialized. More important, however, the budget resolution was based on optimistic economic assumptions that soon proved totally unrealistic. The recession precipitated by high interest rates in 1981 caused a rapid surge in deficits. Financing an escalating debt at high interest rates led to unprecedented increases in federal spending for interest payments. As a result, increases in spending for defense and interest substantially exceeded cuts in domestic spending, leaving a growing deficit even as the economy recovered.

Beginning in 1982, rapidly escalating deficits subjected the entire federal budget process to extreme stress. Under this stress two weaknesses of the decision process stood out clearly: the basic problem, built into the Constitution, of resolving any difficult problem when the president and Congress disagree, and the layering of the process that made it unwieldy and time consuming in normal times and close to nonfunctional under stress.

Difficulties of Divided Power

The debate over each successive budget since 1981 has been dominated by clashes of views over the deficits. Between 1982 and 1984 President Reagan vacillated on the seriousness of the deficits, sometimes alleging that they would disappear as the economy grew and sometimes deploring them and calling for reduced domestic spending. Presidential budget proposals reflected a consistent budget strategy that continued the defense buildup and rejected both tax increases and cuts in social security, but proposed substantial reductions in many domestic activities.

Congressional leaders generally made stronger statements about the necessity of getting the deficits down, but differed with the president and with each other on how to do it. Actual budget actions reflected painfully engineered compromises that generally pared back the president's defense increases, accepted some but by no means all of the proposed domestic cuts, and raised revenues somewhat, most notably in 1982 when aspects of the generous tax cuts of the previous year were rescinded. The result was to reduce anticipated further increases in the deficits but to leave them still at unprecedented levels even though the economy began recovering rapidly in 1983.

By 1985 both the administration and Congress had come to realize that the deficits would not disappear with economic growth and were a threat to the long-run health of the economy. But views on what to do had not converged. The battle over the fiscal 1986 budget was long and bitter. It resulted in congressional rejection of further defense increases in that year and of most of the deep domestic spending cuts proposed by the president. The president first accepted and then pulled away from a Senate-passed proposal to suspend the social security cost-of-living adjustment and similarly rejected all efforts to reduce the deficit by increasing revenues. Although final budget actions made inroads on future deficits, the conflict left all parties feeling frustrated, discouraged, and helpless.

In this atmosphere the Gramm-Rudman-Hollings proposal was offered as an amendment to a necessary increase in the debt ceiling in the fall of 1985 and unexpectedly gained wide support. Although members of his administration expressed reservations about the approach, especially about the possible impact on defense spending, the president endorsed the proposal and it passed quickly.

The impact of the new law was felt immediately. Application of the law's sequestration procedure on a limited basis in fiscal 1986 cut $11.7 billion from spending in that year and reduced the spending base by substantially more than that for future years. As pointed out in chapter 3, however, reaching the targets by applying the law's sequestration formula in 1987 and beyond would seriously impair the effectiveness of both civilian and defense programs. It is hard to believe Congress and the president will allow this to occur. The hope is that the desire to avoid this outcome will bring Congress and the president into agreement on a more sensible way of reaching the targets.

The current situation is complicated, however, by the possibility that the Supreme Court may uphold a circuit court ruling that the sequestration process is unconstitutional because it involves having an officer of Congress (the comptroller general) certify what cuts are to be made by the president. The lower court held this a violation of the constitutional separation of powers. If the Supreme Court upholds the lower court, Congress can still use a procedure in the law that involves voting to sequester the funds specified by the formula. They might be reluctant to do this, however, and if they did, the president could veto.

Even if it forces agreement on a deficit reduction plan, Gramm-Rudman-Hollings is an undesirable budget process. First, the sequestration procedure, which requires cutting every line item in the budget by a fixed percentage, allows no reconsideration of priorities and could lead to absurd and unintended results. Second, as noted in chapter 2, the adoption of a fixed dollar target for the deficit can lead to destabilizing fiscal policy. If the deficit rises because of a recession, cutting the deficit could make the recession worse.[1]

Finally, the enactment of Gramm-Rudman-Hollings did nothing to reduce the layering and complexity of the current budget process. The law does strengthen enforcement of the budget resolution, which should improve congressional self-discipline, but it also adds to congressional workloads and accelerates deadlines that were already proving impossible to meet. For example, the law requires Congress to pass the budget resolution by April 15, although the current deadline of May 15 has not been met in some years. We believe that an important reason why deadlines are missed is that the process itself is overly complicated. Congress will not solve this problem merely by exhorting itself to try harder to finish on time.

1. An escape clause allows postponement of attempts to achieve the target in a recession but requires returning to the target as soon as the economy begins to grow again. This could choke off recovery.

Simplifying the Budget Process

Even before it was subjected to the stress of dealing with large deficits and divergent views among House, Senate, and president, the budget process was showing signs of breaking down of its own weight. Participants complained about the length of time spent on each budget—at least six months for preparation of the president's proposal and at least nine months for congressional decisions. Deadlines were missed regularly, and continuing resolutions became more and more frequent because agreement often could not be reached on regular appropriations. Participants also complained about the multiplicity of congressional committees with overlapping jurisdictions. Testifying on the same issues before several committees on both sides of the Hill consumed the time of executive branch officials and members of Congress alike. Moreover, the frequency of decisions on the same issues meant that many decisions were never final. Crucial votes on major weapons systems, such as the MX missile, were occurring in each house three or more times in a single year in the context of authorization, appropriation, and budget action. Congress seemed more and more immersed in the details of federal programs and less and less concerned with the overall directions of federal policy. A growing number of members and observers of Congress have come to believe that drastic change is needed to improve the effectiveness of the congressional budget process. But the deficit crisis itself has delayed serious consideration of procedural change.

Three types of reform would make effective decisionmaking more feasible: making decisions less often by moving to a multiyear budget, reducing the number of committees by consolidating the authorizing and appropriating processes, and simplifying the budget itself by reducing the number of accounts and line items.

Multiyear Budgeting

An obvious way to reduce the time spent on the budget process would be to go through the process less often, perhaps every other year. Less frequent budgeting has many clear benefits. The managers of federal programs and the recipients of federal grants could plan programs more effectively if they could assume funding for a longer period. They could spend more time managing and less time preparing and defending budgets and adjusting to funding changes. And Congress, relieved of annual budget battles, could devote more attention to long-run issues and more careful oversight of federal programs.

Spending levels for some programs are, of course, affected by unpredictable cataclysmic events, such as the outbreak of war. But such events have to be dealt with on an emergency basis even with an annual budget process. It is hard to imagine that most federal programs benefit more from hasty annual review than from more thorough, better prepared evaluation at longer intervals.

It is true that budgeting depends on economic assumptions about the future and that longer-run forecasts are more uncertain. But only a few programs are greatly affected by the state of the economy, and many of these are entitlement programs that adjust automatically. If the economy suffered an unexpected recession in the middle of the multiyear budget period, Congress might well want to consider changing tax rates or accelerating some spending programs. But this could be done—as it is now—without reconsidering the whole budget.

Numerous bills proposing multiyear budgets have been introduced—most calling for biennial budgeting, which is used by many state governments—and some hearings have been held. Some biennial budget bills envision Congress spending the first year of each session on program oversight and other matters and handling the two-year budget in the second year of the session. Under this arrangement a newly elected president who wanted to alter his predecessor's budget could either use the first year of his term to build support and understanding for the changes or could move ahead more rapidly to amend the existing budget. Other bills would have each Congress make a two-year budget in its first session and use the second for other activities.

Even if the whole budget were not moved to a multiyear basis, Congress could get many of the advantages of multiyear budgeting by shifting to multiyear authorization or appropriation or both in major areas of the budget. Defense seems an especially appropriate area for such a change. Indeed, recent defense legislation takes the preliminary step of requiring the Department of Defense to submit a two-year budget beginning with fiscal years 1988 and 1989.

While congressmen sometimes argue that they would have less control over federal activities if budgeting were done less often, they actually would have more scope for making significant changes. Major shifts in direction, such as bringing down the deficit or modernizing the armed forces, cannot be accomplished in a single year. A longer budgeting period would give greater scope for such major shifts to be designed and carried out. Indeed, in the last several years Congress has of necessity moved to a multiyear budget resolution with accompanying reconciliation measures. The dramatic changes of 1981 involved a three-year budget resolution as well as a three-year tax bill. Subsequent efforts to bring down the deficit necessarily involved more than one year, so three-year budget resolutions have become standard. Nevertheless, appropriations and many authorizations are still done one year at a time. It is time to move the whole process to a two-year cycle.

Consolidating the Authorizing and Appropriating Processes

In principle the legislative or authorizing committees write the basic legislation that governs how federal programs function, and the appropriation committees budget specific sums to carry them out. In practice the distinction between the two has often blurred in recent years, perhaps because of the intensity of interest in the budget and the small number of new programs being considered. In working out the defense budget, for example, the authorizing committees and appropriation subcommittees often appear to be doing exactly the same thing—subjecting the budget to line-by-line scrutiny with special attention to procuring weapons systems. Such duplication wastes the time and energy of Congress and executive branch alike.

On the other hand, spending for entitlements, now two-fifths of the budget, is outside the appropriation process. The bulk of entitlement spending is handled by the tax committees, sometimes creating logjams for these overworked committees.

Restructuring the committees would improve the budget process. Ideally, each major area of federal activity—defense, income security, national resources, and so forth—should have a program committee. These committees would be responsible both for drafting basic legislation and for reviewing budgets in their area. They would handle both entitlement programs and discretionary appropriations. Revenue committees would handle only revenue, not spending programs. The budget committees would be charged with putting together an overall budget strategy that would include both revenue and spending. They would also consider relative priorities among programs and recommend appropriate fiscal policy.

A further step, one with considerable appeal, would be to hold all spending and tax bills for final vote at the same time. Indeed, they could be put into a single bill. Congress would then be voting on a budget for the whole government and sending it to the president at the same time. This type of budget action is standard in many governments, but as noted above, the U.S. government has never had a budget voted this way.

Simplifying the Budget

Under present procedures a single omnibus appropriations bill would be an appallingly long document. This length is symptomatic of a basic problem of the budget process: the tendency of Congress to budget in too great detail. The current budget is divided into thousands of budget accounts and subaccounts. The executive branch is given very detailed line item budgets with little authority to shift money from one item to another as conditions change. This detail makes the budget process an arcane business and focuses congressional time and energy on minutia rather than on overriding issues of policy.

Drastically cutting the number of line items in the budget would be desirable but would only make a real difference if accompanied by a genuine change in the way Congress perceives its own role. Congress would have to begin functioning more like a board of directors making major policy decisions for the country and less like a group of 535 managers specifying detailed operations for the executive branch.

Political Opposition

None of the changes suggested here would require amending the Constitution. Each could be accomplished by legislation or changes in House and Senate rules and customary practice. All the recommendations, however, would meet with strong opposition in Congress (and to some extent in the executive branch) because each threatens the existing power structure. Multiyear budgeting would deprive Congress of the annual chance to impose its will in appropriations and other budget legislation. Consolidating the authorization and appropriation processes would reduce the number of committee and subcommittee chairmanships. Budgeting in less detail is perhaps the most threatening of all because Congress has a long tradition of making itself felt and protecting constituent interest through tinkering with line items. Nevertheless, Congress is highly frustrated with the current system, which imposes an exhausting workload but yields little satisfaction of accomplishment. Once the deficit crisis is at least partially resolved, but before memories of this stressful period recede, the chance for substantial reform of the budget process seems high.

Other Possible Procedural Reforms

President Reagan favors two major changes in budget procedures that he believes would work to hold down federal spending and deficits: a constitutional amendment to require a balanced budget and a line item presidential veto.

While we share the president's desire to reduce the current deficits, we believe that requiring balance in the budget regardless of the state of the economy could force the federal government to adopt an inappropriate fiscal policy. Drafts of constitutional amendments usually have escape clauses, but it is difficult to foresee the variety of special circumstances that could affect future fiscal policy. Such amendments usually empower a super majority (two-thirds or three-fifths of Congress) to override a requirement to balance the budget. Such a clause, however, might create an incentive for legislators with favorite spending projects to trade the inclusion of these projects for their agreement to join the super majority. Spending and deficits might actually end up larger than without the amendment. To the extent that an amendment to balance the budget holds down federal spending, however, it may lead the government to substitute additional regulation for spending and to achieve goals by requiring businesses or state and local governments to make certain kinds of expenditures. Such amendments also provide a strong incentive to create off-budget agencies or engage in "creative" accounting. All in all, the risk of trying to handle a complex issue like fiscal policy by amendment to a Constitution whose greatest virtue is its brevity and flexibility seems far greater than the benefits.

The proposed line item veto also presents problems. While the president may use his veto power only to reject a whole bill, many state governors have the power to veto individual line items. Numerous presidents have asked for line item veto power in order to forestall the congressional tendency to insert spending items with which the president disagrees into bills he needs and does not want to veto.

The line item veto would enhance the power of the president and diminish that of Congress, but it is easy to exaggerate its impact. The president needs congressional support for his programs and is unlikely to risk antagonizing many members, especially chairmen of important committees and subcommittees. Moreover, the latter could doubtless find ingenious alternative ways of protecting favorite line items, such as military bases or other federal installations, from presidential veto. A committee could hide a threatened line item in a larger total, for example, and add language stating that none of the funds are to be used to close the specified installation. Moreover, while a conservative president might use a line item veto to cut pork barrel spending projects, a big-spending president might use the threat of a line item veto to garner votes for spending he favored.

In any case it is not realistic to think that the line item veto would reduce the current deficit appreciably. President Reagan is unlikely to use a line item veto to reduce defense spending. Interest payments cannot be vetoed, and entitlement programs generally do not come to the president in a form in which such a veto would be possible. The president might use the line item veto to kill a few domestic spending items of largely local interest, but the spending impact of such actions would be small.

Conclusion

Simplifying the budget process along the lines we have discussed would make the process more understandable and less exhausting and would probably lead to more thoughtful decisions. It is important, however, not to claim too much for procedural change. A well-designed budget process can, at best, do three things. It can reduce but not eliminate uncertainty by making sure that participants have the best available projections and analyses of budget options in intelligible form. It can also put the sequence of decisions in a logical order so that participants have a chance to make the most important decisions, not just the subsidiary ones. This lack of order was the weakness in the congressional budget process corrected by the reforms of 1974. Finally, a well-designed budget process can save time for decisionmakers so that budget affairs do not overwhelm other activities of government. The current process fails miserably on this last criterion.

No set of procedures, however, can force participants to make choices that they do not want to make or do not regard as necessary. Reforms to the process cannot substitute for political will or for the exercise of leadership in working out compromises among warring parties. As long as the government sticks with a system under which power is divided between the president and Congress—and we would not counsel abandoning the separation of powers—the priorities of the president and Congress will occasionally conflict. Changes in budget process are unlikely to cure this situation. Resolution of the conflict will still require statesmanship and the willingness of both sides to compromise.

DATE DUE